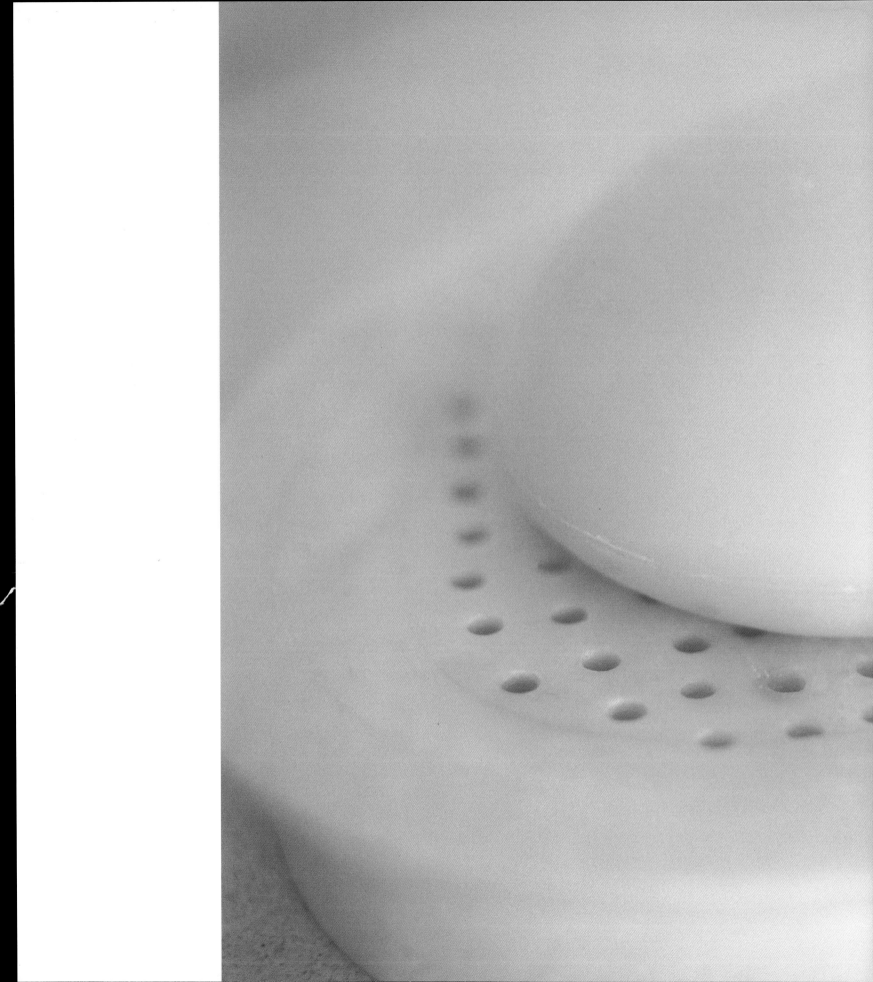

sensual living

CLAIRE LLOYD

TEXT BY ROS BYAM SHAW

conran
OCTOPUS

To my Mum and Dad

contents

FOREWORD 10

INTRODUCTION 11

SMELL 12

TOUCH 28

TASTE 48

SIGHT 60

SOUND 83

SIXTH SENSE 97

INDEX 158

ACKNOWLEDGMENTS 160

FOREWORD BY CLAIRE LLOYD

Everyone has their own interpretation of sensual living, so this is a very subjective topic. To me, it means the ways in which you use what is around you to touch on all your senses, and it is this that I am presenting in this book – my interpretation of sensual living.

There are some very basic elements that will always remain sensual for me, and there are some others that could change in time. I know, for example, that I cannot live without a lot of natural light so the idea of blinds or curtains fills me with horror. Likewise, I surround myself with a tidy environment or I can't be clear in my thoughts; and, finally, each object in my house, whether it be a sofa or a glass, has to stand on its own as a piece that gives my senses pleasure.

Not only does this book show what sensual living means to me, it is also a guide to you as to how this can be achieved once you understand what is around you and why you like it. Without touch there is no feeling; without sight, no visual difference, no colour, no pattern. Being deprived of taste and smell would mean the loss of the delicious and the fragrant. Our environment is made up of so many elements and there is always an opportunity to make them work for us and our well-being. Our senses make up our whole being. They give us enjoyment and pleasure, peace and tranquillity, excitement and delight, and I hope that the simple ideas found within these pages will inspire you to gain pleasure from what surrounds you and your senses.

INTRODUCTION BY ROS BYAM SHAW

Most books about domestic style concentrate on appearances; modish minimalism, cottagey clutter; a grouping of pots; an arrangement of elegant simplicity on a mantelpiece; here is colour, shape, form, light and shade. These are the dimensions of a picture on a page. This is a world where looks are all-important, where the visual reigns supreme. They are, in a sense, just that, merely visual, made for the selfish eye.

The best photographs transcend the visual, hinting at how an interior might feel to the touch; the warmth of a sunlit patch on a wooden floor, the cool satin of stainless steel. At their most evocative, photographs of a room may remind you of a scent, or a sound, or even a taste like the tang of salt air.

This book, too, is bound by the limitations of paper and print. Even the pyrotechnics of virtual reality have yet to include any of our senses beyond sight and sound. But, although in these pictures you cannot smell, or taste, touch or hear the waves, the flowers and stone, the fruit and sand, the linen and leather, this is a book about the importance and interplay of all our senses in the domestic environment and each image has been chosen because its reality appeals to more than one of them. A well-constructed, well-designed interior may do much more than merely gratify the eye.

Le Corbusier's ideal of the house as a 'machine for living' and armchair as 'machine for sitting in' has had a profound influence on late twentieth-century design. But instead of interpreting this idea through technology to construct 'machines' that perfectly suit our needs, the word 'machine' is often translated to mean that which has a look of industrial robustness, that which can be mass-produced. This is the same visual hegemony that favours raw cement over stone, chrome over wood. Modernism in its pure form is still a rare manifestation, but its influence has filtered down to much contemporary design and its emphasis on looks as opposed to comfort has persisted.

Where the filtering has formed a sediment at the level of high-street merchandise we see small, slippery rugs on big slippery floors, twisting iron furniture round glass-topped tables and sofas that chicly defy you to lie back and enjoy yourself with a sneer of their taut little curves. It is all very well to cut a swagger but for enduring appeal you need more than good looks. The failure of much modern design to engage us physically, beyond the visual, may be one explanation for the enduring popularity of period style in interior design. We turn to the past partly because some furnishings of the eighteenth and nineteenth centuries offer more than dogma. As we approach the end of the century there are signs that we are changing the aspect of our interiors – shaking off some of the constrictions of modernism, re-thinking our priorities, even sinking back on our sofas.

The pleasure to be derived from our homes is dependent on all our senses. When we escape the strictures of an overly visual aesthetic, we instinctively cater for them. Before we decide to buy a fabric, we appreciate its texture, touch it, stroke it, weigh it in our hands; we might even rub it against our cheek and sniff it. When we choose a floor covering, we kneel on it, run our palms over it, push a foot across it. We collapse into chairs, knead cushions, bounce on beds, open and close doors, before we choose and buy. Not having the opportunity to do this is one of the insuperable disadvantages of catalogue shopping.

Sound and smell are generally lower on our agenda. This is probably because their effects tend to be more subliminal although no less profound. When we speak of not liking the 'atmosphere' of a house or room, we may be reacting against its sounds and smells without realizing the sources of our dislike. Conversely, the soothing and seductive effects of good smells and sweet sounds hardly need advertising. Yet all too often we forget about them when planning a room and designing an interior.

In this book, there are no period recreations, no ersatz country-house interiors, no chintzy sofas or fake farmhouse kitchens. In the houses and rooms shown here there is comfort and there is pleasure; pleasure for the eyes but also for the hands, feet and skin; pleasure for the nose and taste-buds, and pleasure for the ears.

Our homes are our retreats, the environment where we feel most safe and in control, the place where we can choose the music we listen to and the scent of the bubbles that pillow our bath. At home, our pleasure is in our own hands. There are as many ways of providing it as there are people to experience it. This book can only explore a tiny fraction of the possibilities, but it is meant to inspire and encourage enjoyment. Nor is it a frivolous goal. The sense of security and relaxation that arise from domestic well-being are deep human needs. Sensual living is about recognizing and answering those needs.

SMELL

He who ruled scent ruled the hearts of men.

PATRICK SUSKIND
Perfume

Leather upholstery exudes a warm subtle scent, the smell of clean animal and polish that lingers inside luxury cars and expensive shoe-shops.

RIGHT: *Fresh fish make a more pungent assault on the nose – the salty tang of the ocean, recalling childhood holidays, beaches and sea breezes.*

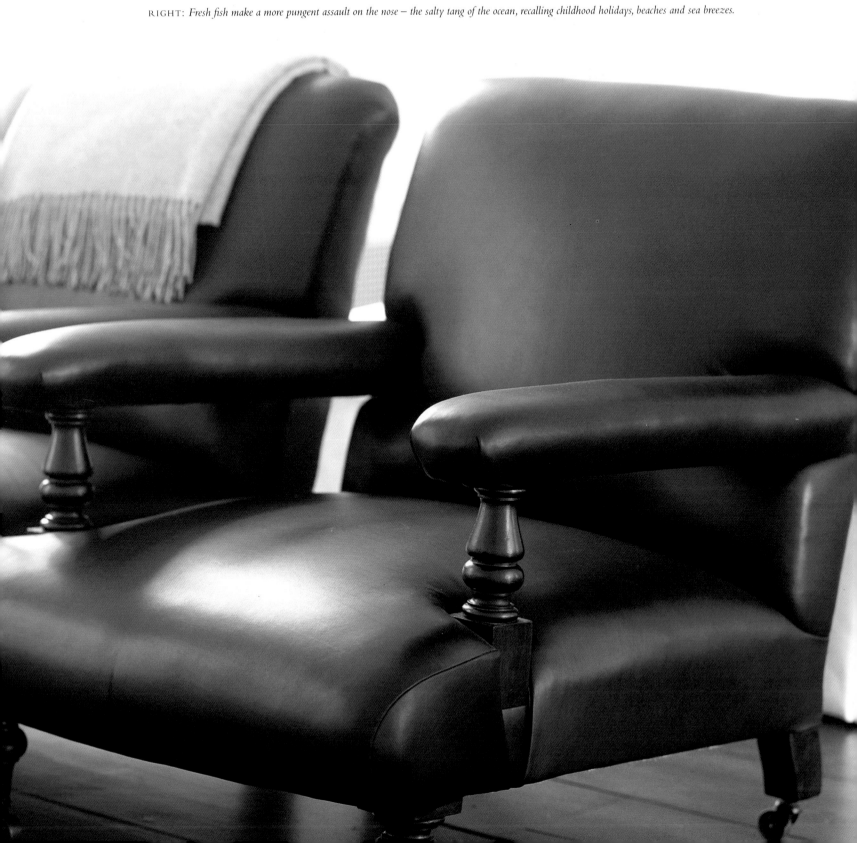

Where sight is precious, smell is primal. It is the sense that brings us closest to our animal ancestry. As civilization has progressed, our sense of smell has become less obviously useful. We no longer need to use our noses when hunting, or deciding when a mate is at her most fertile. But our sense of smell remains intimately connected with these, our most basic and instinctual pleasures, food and sex. To fill our houses with good smells is to give ourselves pleasures at once apparent and subliminal.

When we breathe, we smell and messages received by our olfactory membranes are powerful whether we recognize their influence or not. A bad smell can, literally, make you sick. Throughout the eighteenth and nineteenth centuries, there was a conviction that evil 'miasmas' were the cause of a whole range of fatal illnesses. But a good smell is another matter. What greater pleasure can there be than to bury your nose in the *honeyed caress* of a primrose, or the soft, warm nape of a baby's neck? Good smells not only influence our choices of partners, and possibly friends, and our choice of nutrition, they have a deep connection with enjoyment of many kinds.

Not to like the smell of someone is probably not to like the person. Conversely, smell is one of the most *powerfully erotic tools of seduction.* Without realizing it, we continue to use the genital and under-arm hair that traps the sexual scents produced by our apocrine glands by, for example, lifting our arm towards a person of the opposite sex we wish to attract. Watch the body language of a couple flirting and you will see this gesture repeated time and again.

In this respect we are decidedly more repressed than our ancestors who lived surrounded by a symphony of stenches, hard to imagine in our deodorized, sanitized age. The waving handkerchief of the latter-day morris dancer dates to a time when an amorous suitor would tuck it in his armpit until soaked with fresh sweat from the rigours of the dance, and then present it to the woman of his desire as a love-token.

We are now more subtle about the scented signals we send but the smell of the skin of someone we love is *deeply alluring.* A mother recognizes the smell of her new-born baby within half an hour of birth, assuming there has been no separation. The baby takes a little longer; forty-five hours after first laying its head against her skin, it will have learnt to identify its mother closely by her body fragrance alone. Children who have not yet accepted the social niceties associated with cleanliness complain bitterly when their security blanket is washed, finding it at its most comforting when it smells, sometimes a little too strongly of their own skin and dried dribble.

While smell has tended to remain at the bottom of the hierarchy of the senses because of its animal associations, there is increasing scientific evidence of its subliminal power. Research at the University of Bern suggests that we are attracted by the smell of a person whose immune system is genetically coded to resist different diseases from our own. In other words, when choosing a partner, we are at the mercy of a primitive 'smell brain' which is programmed to choose a mate with more resistance to more diseases. Discoveries like these go a long way towards explaining 'love at first sight', which should perhaps be more accurately described as 'love at first sniff'.

The power of smell to affect us on an unconscious level is the theme of Patrick Suskind's best-selling novel *Perfume,* which tells of a pauper born in the slums of eighteenth-century Paris. Grenouille is possessed of two extraordinary qualities: he completely lacks a personal body odour, and has a sense of smell so exquisitely refined that he can distinguish the scent of the girl he plans to murder at a distance of several miles. The book takes the putative tyranny of smell to an extreme which is only believable because we instinctively recognize its basis in truth. When Suskind describes how Grenouille goes unnoticed about his crimes we accept that his very lack of smell is his best protection. When Grenouille improvises a perfume that gives him the human smell he lacks, using a base which includes cat excrement, vinegar, mouldy cheese and singed pork rink, subsumed under a layer of fresh and floral scents, we may feel offended, but not incredulous.

Suskind's book is a tour de force on the power of smell, and it is a remarkable caricature of human nature. But Grenouille's belief in the *irresistible force of smell* which 'entered human beings, who could not defend themselves against it', and which 'went directly to their hearts', has more than a grain of truth.

The relationship between food and smell is less fraught. Much of our pleasure in what we think of as taste is actually due to our sense of smell. When we lose our sense of smell with a cold, our sense of taste is hugely diminished. Smell also provides an essential early warning system which helps to protect our stomachs against bacteria and poisons. We sniff our food before tasting, not just for the pleasure of it but as a test of its wholesomeness, checking that the milk hasn't gone off or that the meat is still fresh.

Nature is generous in the abundance and variety of her scents. Flowers possess an incredible range of different and delicious odours, from the thick, heady perfume of a lily to the sweet evanescence of

RIGHT: *Soothing scents mingle in a bathroom; the sweet, clean comfort of a laundered towel; a favourite soap, a few sprigs of jasmine and a perfumed candle.*

ABOVE: *A small leather suitcase offers more than simple good looks; carry it with you and you have a portable source of olfactory pleasure, like the scent you wear, or a modern version of the pomander.*

RIGHT: *The syrupy aroma of ripe melon is an invitation to taste, sending messages to the brain that set the mouth watering, ready to eat. Even inside the mouth, where its sweetness is registered by the taste buds, the subtleties of its characteristic fruity flavour will be largely experienced by the nose.*

freesias. In a wonderfully generous coincidence of nature, the very scents manufactured by flowers to attract insects to pollinate them are as delectable to us as they are to bumble-bees and butterflies. Thanks to their manoeuvrings for survival, there are even flowers that save their perfume for our enjoyment after an alfresco dinner: honeysuckles and night-scented stocks, which release their scents at twilight, luring moths with faces that almost glow in the quiet gloom of a summer's evening.

Freshly cut flowers in crystal-clear water bring some of nature's loveliest scents indoors. A few flowers, like lavender – one of summer's most evocative scents – retain much of their sweetness when dried, and can fill a cupboard with the most delicious smell of sunshine.

Herbs invite the taste buds with rich and tangy scents. A small pot of basil on a warm windowsill breathes a spice from its leaves as irresistible to the nose as to the tongue.

Not content with the sweetness of smells that come free, since the earliest civilizations man has attempted to trap and capture the best smells, to adorn his own body and perfume his environment. Scented plants have long been valued for their therapeutic and medicinal qualities, beliefs that have been revitalized and given renewed credence by the growing popularity of aromatherapy. In 4500BC the emperor of China, Kiwant Ti, wrote a medical book about the properties of plants. The Ancient Egyptians used perfumes in magic and religious ceremonies and for the processes of embalming. Women wore scented wax cones on their heads which gradually melted in the heat of the day, cooling their hair and releasing their perfume. The Hebrews used *incense and aromatic oils* to repel evil spirits and the Greeks used natural plant essences as perfumes and for body care. Hippocrates attempted to arrest the spread of the plague in Athens by arranging aromatic fumigations on the streets.

Scents made from distillations of plants were difficult and time-consuming to produce. If ingredients were not locally available, they had to be shipped from their country of origin, adding hugely to their expense and rarity. When the wife of the Roman Emperor Nero died he used as much incense at her funeral as was produced in Arabia in the course of ten years. It was also Nero who, with utmost extravagance,

installed in his palace a series of ivory plates hiding silver pipes which could spray a variety of perfumes on assembled guests. Elizabeth I had her palaces *sprinkled with rose-water* – also an extraordinary extravagance when you consider that it takes 100 kg (224 lb) of rose petals to produce between 50 and 80 grams (2 and 3 oz) of essential oil. And no list of royal indulgence would be complete without a mention of Versailles where Louis XV required all members of the court to adopt a different perfume each day of the week.

The best scents are still an expensive luxury, their production shrouded in a mystique encouraged by their makers. Scientific formulae have largely taken over from traditional recipes, but the skill of the 'nose' who mixes and blends them always remains paramount. When we find a scent that complements our skin, that *mellows, softens and harmonizes* with our own smell, we carry the pleasure of that smell with us all day. To find the scent that suits us best and wear it consistently gives it the status of a personal hallmark. Even though scents are subtly different on everyone, the smell of a particular scent is the most tantalizing reminder of a person who wears it wherever a whiff of its aroma is caught.

Just as artists have always been sensitive to colour's emotional power, poets and novelists have used descriptions of smell to emphasize polarities of desire and disgust. Shakespeare imagines the barge of his definitive femme fatale, Cleopatra, with sails 'so perfumed that/The winds were love-sick with them'. For the romantic poets scent was a vehicle for the mysteries of memory, love and reverie.

The writer whose minute observations most perfectly capture the virtually indescribable links between perception, memory and emotion is Proust. At the beginning of the first volume of his epic novel, *A la Recherche du Temps Perdu*, he makes the observation; 'when from a long-distant past nothing subsists, after the people are dead, after the things are broken and scattered, taste and smell alone, more fragile but more enduring, more immaterial, more persistent, more faithful, remain poised a long time, like souls, remembering, waiting, hoping, amid the ruins of all the rest; and bear unflinchingly, in the tiny and almost impalpable drop of their essence, the vast structure of recollection'.

LEFT: *The scent of a flower is its means of survival, designed to seduce insects for pollination.* ABOVE: *Fruit uses scent for similar purposes, to encourage consumption and the spread of its seeds. In this case, we are more appropriate targets, and just as susceptible to the smell of a pear as the birds who feast in the branches of its tree.*

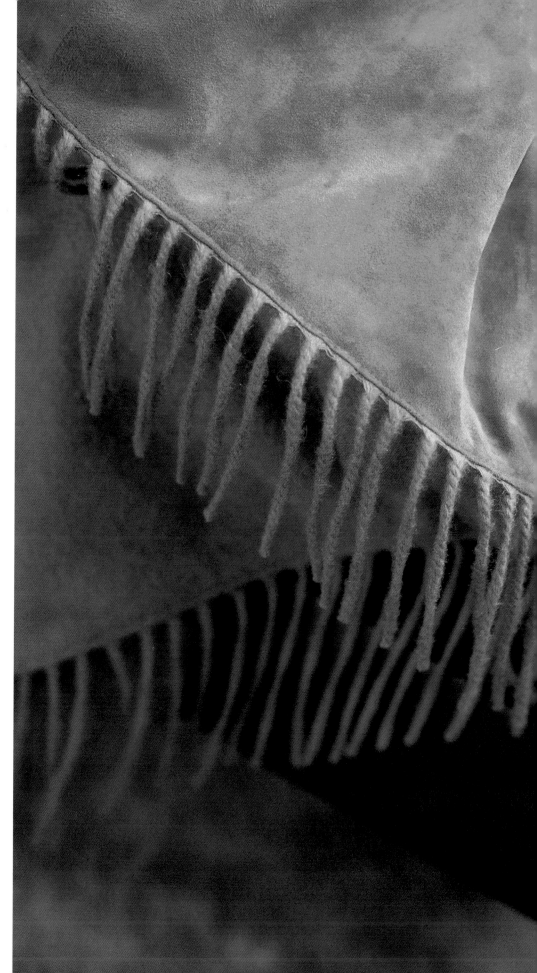

ABOVE: *Linen, washed and starched, crisp and heavy, has a fresh, old-fashioned smell that speaks of time and care spent on domestic details, conveying a sense of homely order that is the essence of security and comfort.*

RIGHT: *A generous shawl in suede, leather's supple sister, can drape a chair or a shoulder, its seductive softness against cheek or nose affording the added pleasure of its faintly musky scent.*

FAR RIGHT: *The complementary aromas of hot coffee and chocolate are at least as delectable as the experience of their consumption.*

So it is, as a grown man, that the experiences of his senses of smell and taste take him back to his childhood at Combray. These are the links that sew together his immense literary survey of his own life and the imagined lives of others with which it overlapped.

Proust found a language to convey experiences which, although common to us all, have a tendency to evade the bonds of words and sentences. Everyone has experienced a so-called 'Proustian rush' – the waft of over-cooked cabbage and mashed potato that takes us back to the school dinner queue; *an old-fashioned cologne* that recalls the rouged peachiness of a grandmother's cheek. Memories and associations appear, vividly recreated whether we want them to or not.

The evocative power of smell, added to the simple enjoyment of inhaling any scent that we love, can be harnessed and utilized to make our homes and gardens places of pleasure for the nose. Thanks to the everyday conveniences of running water, flushing lavatories and efficient refuse collection and disposal, most of us start with the blank canvas of relatively fresh air. Town and city dwellers may complain about the evils of pollution but, although it is a problem that should rightly be addressed, at least there is no need to block up letterboxes to stop the invasion of 'pea-soupers' that regularly blanketed London and other cities in a cloud of thick smog as recently as the 1950s. And not only is urban air cleaner than it has ever been, so are our bodies.

Still warm from the branch, a lemon carries its fragrance in the oil of its skin and the gloss of its leaves.

For our ancestors, good smells were primarily used to mask bad. Herbs were strewn among the straw that covered floors in rooms next to latrines. Pomanders were carried ready to be held against the nostrils whenever a particularly foul stench threatened. Body scents were extra pungent – and often overtly sexual with their tang of musk and civet – to be apparent above the smells of dirty bodies and unwashed clothes. Incense in churches was as much a means of fumigation as a religious ritual. Even in Versailles, where perfumes were taken so seriously, the corridors were regularly urinated in by servants and courtiers alike.

Other smells that were thought unacceptable by our ancestors are still censured. Queen Victoria banned smoking in all her homes, while other, more liberal, hostesses banished cigar-smokers to smoking rooms. While there are still those who rank a fat cigar or leisurely cigarette as one of life's great sensual pleasures, stale tobacco smoke is truly one of the more noxious odours of modern life.

Different smells are suitable for different rooms. A woman's scent may pervade her bedroom, clinging to clothes, *a personal signature*. Soaps and bath oils leave their airy mark in bathrooms. A blazing log fire fills a living room with the comforting whiff of wood smoke. Scented candles combine soothing light with soft smells.

Of all the rooms in a house, the kitchen is likely to be the source of the strongest and some of the most delicious smells. Right until the twentieth century, Anglo-Saxon societies tended to consider kitchen smells unacceptable in other rooms, and so they separated the functions of cooking from the rest of the house by as much distance as wealth and space allowed. Town houses relegated kitchens to basements, while large country houses exiled them to a wing that was separated by long corridors from the main reception rooms. The inevitable corollary of cold food was less unpleasant than the leaking of unwanted odours. Mediterranean cultures, in contrast, *took pleasure* in the spread of cooking smells, building their houses around central courtyards where the scents of food, often from more than one kitchen, would collect and mingle. Afro-Caribbeans have a similarly relaxed approach to food preparation, taking pleasure in the spicy mix of kitchen odours.

Today, throughout Europe and North America the kitchen has assumed a new place in the hierarchy of rooms, and cookery has become a leisure activity. Contemporary architects rarely cordon off a kitchen, preferring instead to fit its working areas into part of a larger room doubling as dining room and living room. Consequently, its smells are no longer contained and instead they have become an acceptable component of domestic comfort. The scent of fresh food, whether it is sizzling garlic or the sweetness of *slow baking meringue*, can be savoured. Stale or over-strong smells can be spirited away by the extractor fan.

Beneath the added overtones of the smells that relate to the daily activities of cooking and washing, and the scents of the people who live in a house, lie the base notes that arise from the materials used to build and furnish it. In India, turned banister rails are made of *cedarwood that releases its soft perfume* as the hand slides along it. Scrubbed flagstones give off a faint mineral odour reminiscent of damp moorland walks. Rush matting and seagrass retain the sweet scent of mown hay. Pure wool never quite looses its whiff of warm animal. Brick that is heated by the sun has an earthy smell, thatch dripping with rain has a vegetable one. Oiled teak, limed oak, tanned leather and linseed-soaked linoleum; each has its own distinctive smell. These are the intrinsic scents of a house that seep from its very fabric. These are the smells that give a place its own identity. They combine to create a unique and subtle recipe that informs the atmosphere of your home and permanently distinguishes it from any other.

Unlike sensualists of the eighteenth century who had actively to seek out the experience of fresh air by travelling far away from their stinking cities and insalubrious villages, we can enjoy a *delicious scent for its own sake* almost anywhere without our noses being bombarded by other, less welcome, sensations. We no longer need dread crowded public places for their miserable, fetid stink, and inside our houses we are masters of the smells they enclose, not martyrs to poor drainage and inadequate water supply. Few of us would go as far as Nero in the orchestration of our home-grown smells, but the scope for olfactory delight is immense and unending.

ABOVE: *The warm spice of basil is also best appreciated freshly picked; a feast for eyes, nose and tongue.*

Onions and toast, two cosy kitchen smells that

epitomize the comforts of good food.

TOUCH

And forget not that the earth delights to feel your bare feet and the winds long to play with your hair.

KAHLIL GIBRAN
The Prophet

Wrapped around our bodies is a silken armour with extraordinary powers. Thin, strong, stretchy and waterproof, our skin is the interface between us and the environment. When damaged, it replaces itself. When exposed to sunlight, it protects itself. It produces moisture for cooling, antiseptic and oils as a barrier against germs. Nor does it only protect. All over its surface are thousands of nerve endings through which we experience infinite modulations of pressure and temperature, pain and pleasure, 'The splash of sun, the shouting wind/ And the brave sting of rain'.

Maintenance of this sensory armour is important to us, as it is to all animals. The cosmetics industry spends millions developing, and makes more millions selling, the creams and lotions that promise to reduce cellulite, wrinkles, spots, blemishes, dryness, greasiness and any other physical inconvenience that comes between us and the perfection of *smooth, soft skin.* Recapturing the inimitable blush of a baby's skin, as finely textured as the petal of a rose is, sadly, a hopeless quest. But even grown-up skin, clean, warm and well-cared-for, has a feel that we love against our own skin more than any other.

Grooming is both a necessity and a pleasure. According to Desmond Morris, we have replaced the important social aspects of mutual grooming, so characteristic of other primates, with 'grooming talk', the kind of superficial chit-chat of the cocktail party or bus-stop. But we have also found ways to satisfy our physical grooming instincts. Because it would be dangerously erotic to fiddle with one another's hair on a casual basis, we have formalized the activity by appointing professionals to do it for us. A visit to the hairdresser is more an indulgence than an imperative for most of us. Massages, manicures, body-wraps and the whole range of other beauty treatments play a similar role.

We enjoy being stroked and massaged and having our hair brushed just as we enjoy the acts of caressing and grooming. Pets with strokable fur offer an irresistible opportunity for *tactile indulgence.* Running a hand down the warm, soft back of a purring animal is as relaxing for the owner as it is nice for the cat. Fur coats and animal skin rugs have a similar appeal and fortunately have been so perfectly recreated by synthetics that we can enjoy their feel without guilt. And we still talk of 'rubbing each other up the wrong way', or 'scratching each other's backs', even though, outside the bedroom, we rarely do either. Babies and small children, not yet accustomed to the experience of their senses, spend a lot of time and energy exploring how things feel. As well as endless manipulation with their hands, of sand, or the bath sponge, or the car keys, they use their lips and tongue, both of which have a disproportionate share of sensory organs, to discover the difference between smooth and gritty, hard and soggy. Babies and small children also like nothing more than taking their clothes off and playing naked. Free from the constraints of modesty, they take unselfconscious pleasure in *exploring the sensations of touch* over their whole body surface.

Adults have lost much of this curiosity and, with it, a certain awareness. There is also an increase in physical inhibition that confines most social contact to a brisk hand shake or fleeting social kiss. Even these brief touches could soon be abandoned by some as too risky. Recent research in America has unearthed a widespread phobia about germs in public places, leading people to avoid touching anything that might have been handled by strangers. Compared with our childhoods of cuddles and mud pies, adult life can be sadly lacking in tactile pleasure. Rediscovering the delights afforded by our sense of touch is to rediscover some of those childhood joys.

Even in the absence of a pet, or a pet masseuse, our homes allow us unlimited scope for satisfying the tactile sense. Domestic comfort depends on the provision of texture to soothe and to stimulate our skin and on varied degrees of support as a means of *relaxing our bodies.* If our bed is too hard, or too soft, like Goldilocks, we find it difficult to *sink into sleep.* If the blankets are itchy, or the pillows too lumpy we feel irritated. We like chairs that are soft enough to cushion our bones and firm enough to support our backs. We like our towels to be fluffy and absorbent and our baths to be smooth.

Before exploring the pleasures afforded by surface contact, it is worth considering those aspects that are concerned with the very substances which surround us. The quality of the air we breathe is registered by our skin. Consequently, if the air is too hot, or too cold, too humid, too dry or too still, we feel uncomfortable. Central heating may be an effective way of keeping our houses warm, but it can also leave us gasping if it is not counterbalanced by a suitable level of moisture. Similarly, bad air-conditioning, that is designed to keep us cool, may contain too high a level of carbon monoxide, air ions and foul odours. Even sunlight in an enclosed room can be oppressive if you aren't able to open the windows. Conversely, *a cool breeze of fresh air* on a hot day or the glow of an open fire on a cold one are pleasures that are both simple and profound.

RIGHT: *The fabrics we choose to wear next to our skin can either stroke or scratch, soothe or irritate. A jumper knitted in smooth, fine cotton wraps a body in softness; the fluffy globe of an allium invites us to cup gentle hands around its petals.*

Water provides some of our favourite sensations and is as essential to existence as air; without it our bodies dehydrate and we die, and far more quickly than if deprived of food. There are strong physiological grounds for believing that our ancestors went through an aquatic stage somewhere between four and seven million years ago. We still retain features such as our flexible spine, partial webbing between our fingers, subcutaneous fat and a direction of hair growth that would be consistent with an existence spent partly in water. Certainly we feel very at home in water. Babies born under water are relaxed and content, and even children just a few months old can be taught to swim without fear. Playing in and near water is one of our most popular leisure activities, the focus of our holidays. Beaches and their accompanying watery activities have an allure that cannot simply be put down to a desire for a tan and a yen to build sand castles.

To have a house on the beach, or with its own swimming pool, or a river or a lake, or even a tiny stream running through its grounds, is to have *an enviable source of sensory pleasure*. Dangling a toe or a hand in running water is irresistible. Diving into a cool pool is to enjoy one of the greatest escapes from a blazing sun. Swimming naked is sheer, delicious hedonism.

Architects over the centuries have exploited this delight of water in some of our loveliest buildings. Courtyards with fountains and pools at their centre characterized the finest Roman villas of Pompeii and Herculaneum and were later a motif in Moorish architecture, most gloriously exemplified in the palace of the Alhambra with its long ponds and tinkling fountains. Reflections in still water redouble the beauty of buildings such as the Taj Mahal or Japan's Golden Pavilion in Kyoto, and, when moats were no longer a defensive necessity, no great European country house was complete without its setting pierced with lakes and fountains.

The appeal is an enduring one. Water constantly remains a favourite focal point for public spaces. Town squares, shopping malls and the atria of grand office buildings all have their obligatory 'water features', while Frank Lloyd Wright's house, known as 'Falling Water', which is built over a natural waterfall, remains a fine model of all that is best in contemporary domestic architecture.

Even without these advantages of architecture and location, most of us are fortunate enough to have ready access to running water; such ready access that we largely take it for granted, perhaps only appreciating the luxury it affords when some technical problem interrupts the supply

PREVIOUS PAGE:

Long ago we lost our own, but still we covet the fur of other animals; sleek cow-hide covering a chaise-longue; the feathery touch of a mohair shawl; wool, woven to make thick, warm blankets; a sheepskin rug with its deep pile.

LEFT: *Desirable pets are those we can stroke. Fake fur, used here for rugs and cushions, is similarly soothing to the touch. Eyes and skin enjoy contrasting textures – old leather; glass, cool and icy; the hairy weave of coarse linen,* TOP RIGHT; *the baby-soft down of a cashmere cushion,* BOTTOM RIGHT.

and we again have to fetch and carry it in buckets from standpipes, like our ancestors and like those in parts of the world where water is still a rare and precious commodity.

It is hard to think of any activity more relaxing than lying in a hot bath, or more invigorating than being pummelled by a cold shower. Water can *surround and cradle us*, lifting the weight from our bodies, warming us through to the bones. Water pumped through with air can massage us like a thousand tiny hands. And the splash of cold water can wake us up with a shock at once bracing and gentle.

Beyond the pleasures of fresh air and clean water, there are a thousand different tactile experiences that are concerned with the materials that we use to create an interior. For centuries before our own, Western architecture was more concerned with hiding and disguising its bare bones under paint and plaster than with emphasizing their texture. Modernist architects reacted against this attitude as essentially pretentious and instead chose to make a virtue of the materials that were their building blocks. Even on the inner surfaces of their buildings, metal and concrete were left to speak for themselves.

When thoughtfully employed, this resistance to applied decoration led to interiors replete with textural interest. In rooms designed by Frank Lloyd Wright, brickwork is bare, hearths reveal their rough stone construction, wood is left unpainted. Only the concrete floors are coloured. 'I began to see brick as brick. I learned to see concrete or glass or metal each for itself.' Sensitively handled, this appreciation of raw materials in the raw, has an aesthetic that appeals to the eye and the touch; horribly bowdlerized it engenders the fake stone cladding that can turn a suburban interior into a feeble caricature of a Flintstones set.

The legacy of the Modernist architects, whose ideas are still being digested, can be seen in the tremendous popularity of *bare wood and metal* in contemporary interiors. After a flurry of rag-rolling, dragging and sponging, designers are also turning back to plain, matt walls and there has even been a vogue for bare plaster.

As always, we are at the mercy of fashion. But we also have greater choice than ever before. In making these choices it is important to consider their impact on our sense of touch. Rough walls may have the right look of rustic decay but, in a confined space like a corridor or on a tight staircase, they will graze your elbow and catch your clothes. Satin upholstery has a *gorgeously decadent gloss* but can be slippery and hence uncomfortable. Context is what counts. To enjoy a

TOP LEFT: *The human love-affair with water is rekindled every time we wash, whether cradled in the embrace of a bath, or braced under the tingling massage of a shower.*

material at its best is to find a place for it that pleases both eye and skin. Porridge looks appetising in a bowl and not so good on walls. Gravel makes an excellent path but pebble-dash can ruin a façade. To live in tune with one's five senses it is necessary to understand the interplay between not only forms, but materials as well.

Textiles are the most obvious source of tactile experience in the home. Any interior, however minimal, relies on textiles for at least two of our most physically enjoyable daily rituals, washing and going to bed. The fabrics that we choose to sleep in and dry ourselves with are particularly important because, unlike curtains, or even upholstery, they are most likely to come into contact with our naked skin. To step out of a sweet-smelling bath, sink toes into the deep pile of a thick bath mat, wrap yourself in the downy hug of a towel big enough to make you feel as you did when your mother dried you on her knees in a warm bundle, is to feel thoroughly spoilt. Follow this with a sensuous slide between freshly laundered linen sheets, crisp, scented and cool.

In our choice of textiles today we are fortunate to the point of spoiling. Not only can we select from a huge array of textiles, whether synthetic, natural or a mix of both, but all are cheaper than they have ever been. For centuries, the *delicate lustre of silk* was a treat reserved for the fabulously wealthy, its manufacture a secret which was closely guarded by Chinese weavers who treated their cultivated silkworms with such awe and respect that loud voices and talk of death were altogether banned in their sacred presence. Over the centuries, silk has been viewed as a treasure; it was regularly used to pay taxes, and was even the chosen ransom to rescue Rome from the Goths.

Throughout this century, following the patenting of viscose rayon at the end of the nineteenth century, new synthetic materials have regularly been introduced. Nylon was invented in the late 1930s and quickly became popular because of its cheapness and the ease of its care. However, once its novelty had worn off, people began to react against it, not on practical grounds, but because of its feel against the skin. A nylon shirt does absolutely no favours to sweaty armpits, and nylon sheets are slimy and toe-catching.

Today's synthetics, with fabrics such as the polyester microfibre which looks and feels like suede but is completely machine-washable, are designed with touch very much in mind. Some are also capable of extraordinary feats of stain, heat and wrinkle resistance. Many are incredibly strong. Current research may soon result in stress-relieving and *scent-infused fabrics*, or even materials containing medication that can be absorbed through the skin. A combination of chemical invention and the infinite variety of weaves that can be programmed into today's textile machinery continues to produce new and fascinating textures. These innovations have been embraced by the fashion industry but, up to now, largely ignored by interior designers.

In spite of technology we still return to the natural fabrics that were consistently enjoyed by our ancestors – linen, cotton, wool, silk and leather, which remain hard to beat for tactile pleasure. A worn leather armchair with a big velvet cushion offers a contrast of textures that feel as welcoming as they look. A downy *soft cashmere blanket* is feather-light and unexpectedly warm. A woollen rug is rough and cosy, a linen slipcover smooth and cool. The pull of a *heavy tapestry* curtain, lined and interlined, makes a magnificently weighty and effective shield between your room and the elements; the waft of translucent cotton muslin at an open window stirs up its own gentle breeze. Unfolding a generously-sized damask linen napkin gives the most simple meal a true sense of occasion.

Texture, weight and drape give all these fabrics their character. Some *feel warm and enveloping*, some feel light, fresh and cool. In the fairly recent past it was common practice to change curtains and upholstery to suit the season – velvets, damasks, felts and woolwork for winter, cottons and linens for summer. This is not such an impractical idea. Heavy curtains can be taken down for summer when a lightweight Roman blind is all that is needed in their place. Rugs can be rolled up and put away, furry cushions exchanged for ones in lighter, subtly textured fabrics. The simple addition of a linen slipcover over a velvet sofa can instantly change the mood of a room from cosy winter retreat to fresh summer resort.

BOTTOM LEFT: *Beans silky as tiny pebbles run through fingers like pulsing liquid.* ABOVE: *Bare feet on a beach, footsteps cushioned by sand, squeezing itself between tired toes. The freedom of walking without shoes is never felt more keenly than on the beach, with its vivid contrasts between the sun-baked and sea-washed, the rock and the sand.*

PREVIOUS PAGE: *The multifarious textures of nature have an inspiring beauty; the tender fluting of a mushroom's gills finds an echo in the intricate pleating of sumptuous fabrics by Fortuny.*

LEFT: *Tiny pleats are made solid in the rigid structure of a lampshade, its formality setting a visual and tactile counterpoint with the tufted chaos of a deep-pile cushion. Fabrics are a constant source of tactile experience, from the clothes on our backs to the rug underfoot, from the sheets on our beds to the towels on our rails.*

RIGHT: *Decorative objects have their own tactile allure – the silky curves of a vase, the bas-relief of a leaf like a giant, natural braille – pleasing to the eye, but asking to be touched.*

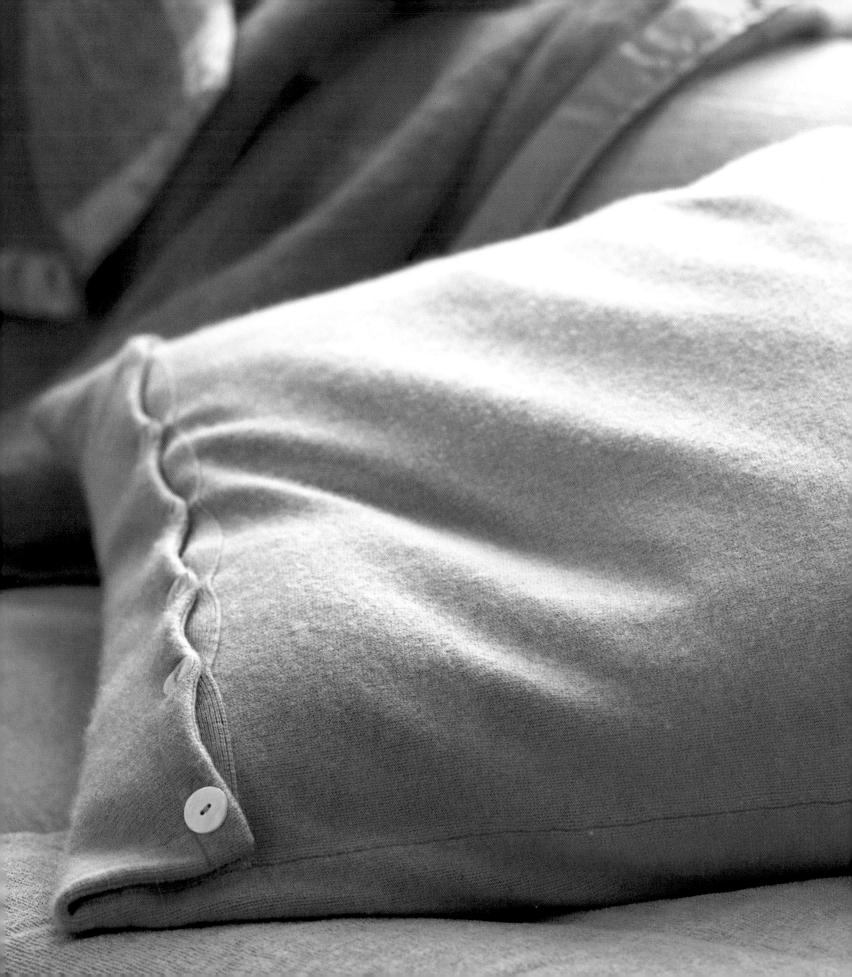

LEFT: *A sofa can be a cocoon, a nest to curl up in, a retreat as safe and soothing as a cuddle. Natural fabrics used here combine the best of warmth and softness – a knitted cashmere cushion, fastened with crisp shell buttons, a mohair blanket for wrapping and draping, its fluffy edges bound with slippery satin – contrast and comfort.*

TOP RIGHT: *The weight, balance and texture of everyday objects, like this metal colander, afford pleasures we largely take for granted.*

MIDDLE RIGHT: *The ancient textures of stone are irresistible to the hand when worn into rounded pebbles by their history of natural attrition.*

BOTTOM RIGHT: *Waffle weave cotton towels have a dimpled texture which is as interesting to look at as it is absorbent around a wet body.*

However fresh the linen or cosy the velvet, we cannot enjoy their qualities if the seat they are covering is the wrong shape. Chairs are an oddly Western phenomenon. Ottoman Turkey, Imperial Persia, Japan and India, for example, felt no need for them. Even in the West chairs existed more as an expression of status than a place of relaxation, until the eighteenth century when the notion of comfort became an issue. During this period, the art of designing a chair, padded for support, its back tilted at the right angle for the spine, its arm-rests also padded, reached a pinnacle. Detailed studies were made of the human body, the aim being to combine the aesthetically pleasing with the physically supportive for maximum comfort.

Further impetus was given to this study towards the end of the next century with the growth of sedentary office work and, by the 1920s, purpose-designed typists' chairs were being manufactured, the form of which has subsequently changed very little. To design a chair that suits every shape, size and weight of body is impossible and, generally, the more infinitely adjustable a seat, the more unattractive its appearance. Car seats are now made adjustable in several dimensions – up, down, back support, head support – but no one would want a group of them around the fireplace, however comfortable.

As babies and children we are particularly alive to sensation — free from inhibitions

we revel in nakedness and the feel of different textures against delicate skin.

Enveloped in a capacious towel, clean, glowing from a bath, we are reminded as adults

of the security and love we felt wrapped up on a parent's knee or folded in a blanket.

Different bodies require different kinds of support and different activities require different postures. Unlike the Romans, who reclined on padded benches to eat, we prefer to sit upright. To read, or watch television, we may want to *curl up in a chair* or lie back on a sofa. The ergonomics of our seating are as important as its appearance and the degree of comfort will be a factor in how relaxed we feel.

One of the largest single surface areas in any room and one which has a major impact on our sense of touch is the floor. In colder countries, where feet are habitually encased in socks and shoes for many months of the year, the delight of walking barefoot is one that is confined to the indoors until summer comes once again. Considering how much weight feet are required to carry and on how small a surface, it is surprising how sensitive they remain.

Bare feet enjoy contrasting textures indoors as much as they do outdoors where they may be walking from gravel to grass or over pebbles to sand. The more violent the contrast, the more dramatic is the effect. A flat-weave rug on floorboards registers subtle changes from the tepid and smooth to the slightly warmer and fibrous; but a deep pile sheepskin on flagstones is like an island of luxury in an ascetic ocean.

Feet are equally sensitive to temperature. A warm floor in a cold climate is particularly comforting. Underfloor heating, especially in bathrooms, is a luxury first invented by the Romans who raised the art of bathing to *new heights of sensory pleasure*. The cool of marble or stone underfoot is a welcome foil to the heat of a summer sun. Cold, hard flooring has always been favoured in hot countries, just as fitted carpets have long been popular in cold ones. Wood fills a comfortable middle ground, hard but without the chill of stone, faintly warm to the touch, but smooth. Soft rugs, strategically placed on wooden floors are as fashionable today as they have ever been, combining a look that is spare but that also provides comfort and contrast.

The vogue for natural materials has prompted a revival in one of the oldest forms of floor covering, rush matting, and of its related natural fibres, jute, sisal and coir. The next step up from strewn rushes, popular in the middle ages for their absorbent qualities, these natural floor coverings have many advantages and some disadvantages. The softest of them, jute, is not particularly hard-wearing, while the tougher coir and sisal have a hairy, prickly feel that grown-up feet may appreciate, but children's knees certainly do not. A combination of matting and rugs is one obvious compromise.

The popularity of these natural floorings has led manufacturers to produce them in ever more varied designs. The different weaves that are available – ribbed, herringbone, tweed, twill and more – provide the visual interest of texture, and range in feel from *pebbly knobbles* to gentle undulations. They are also available dyed in an ever-widening range of colours, but since their popularity is based on their appearance of anti-synthetic, artless simplicity, to try and pretend they are fitted carpets seems a little pointless.

While flooring and fabrics probably provide the greatest quantity of textural experience in an interior, there are a hundred other surfaces that we handle every day in our homes. Furniture, ornaments, work surfaces, equipment, tools, knobs, buttons and handles all come into regular contact with our skin. We may turn a particular door handle dozens of times a day. It may be *rounded glass, or ribbed brass*; small and wooden or large and plastic. How it feels in the hand will only register if it doesn't work well, is too slippery or too stiff. But if it fits into your palm, turns neatly, and feels pleasant, you will experience *a degree of satisfaction* every time you open that door. China, cutlery and glass can afford similar satisfactions when they feel right to hands and lips.

Ornaments are less obvious candidates for handling but you only have to remember the frustration of your last museum visit when you could look but not touch to know how important the feel of an object is, even if it is not to be used. To explore and experience an object fully, the eyes alone are not enough. More information is required which can only be logged when you pick it up, weigh it in your hands and stroke its surface. To date and identify a *piece of porcelain*, an antique dealer will do much more than look. It may be a fake, in which case its weight and the texture of its surface will provide important evidence. It may have been restored, in which case the restoration will feel warmer to the cheek than its original parts. Similarly, you can distinguish between even the finest imitation pearls and the real thing by gently biting one between the front teeth. A real pearl has a hard, almost gritty feel, impossible to fake.

Most of us know our own homes so incredibly well that we could feel our way around them with eyes closed. But, would we necessarily like what we feel? Our sense of touch deserves and demands close attention in the design and detail of our interiors and there are a great many ways to provide it with good feelings.

RIGHT: *The kitchen is full of objects we handle many times a day, objects that must be practical and fit for their purpose, not simply decorative. Cutlery and crockery bring different textures to lips and hands – here the warmth of polished horn contrasts with the hard mineral shine of glazed white china.*

TASTE

For he on honey-dew hath fed
And drunk the milk of Paradise

COLERIDGE

As we pick up a glass of cold white wine, our hands experience the chill of condensation, we inhale the scent of it contents, and then we take a sip. Three of our senses are engaged and stimulated.

Good food is pure pleasure. Sydney Smith's famous definition of heaven entailed 'eating pâté de foie gras to the sound of trumpets'. Keats required more ingredients, 'books… fine weather and a little music out of doors', as well as fruit and wine. In societies where food is plentiful, eating and drinking is an indulgence, an elaborate and ritualized activity, a joy that we relish several times a day. The home naturally forms the back-drop to the rites of food preparation and consumption.

If we simply ate for survival, if our prime motivation was to provide ourselves with nutrition and fuel, we would have changed our habits long ago. Today, most meals could quite feasibly consist of single tablets, speedily swallowed with a nice glass of water; shopping would be so much easier, no heavy bags, no dithering at the cheese counter; the lunch hour would seem so much longer; and slaving over a hot stove would be a distant memory. Astronauts have already tried it, and tired of it.

Without going so far towards nutritional efficiency, we could still save ourselves time by eating our food unprepared, as we might have done when back in the jungle; a meal of peeled hazelnuts, a raw egg, and some chunks of uncooked swede – simple and nourishing. But unless very hungry (and we rarely are) it hardly sets the mouth watering.

Some food is at its best unadulterated. A peach picked and eaten while it is still *warmed with sunshine*, a handful of fresh rocket leaves or an oyster on ice are perfect just as they come. But most of the food we enjoy, even simple staples like rice or bread, has undergone many processes before it reaches our kitchen and we are highly likely to subject it to many more before it reaches our plates.

We heat and cook food, not simply as a safety measure to kill bacteria, but to enhance or alter its flavour, texture or temperature. We freeze ice cream for the sake of contrast and enjoy the sensation of its sharp chill on our tongue. We add yeast to bread to make it feel fluffy in our mouths. We sprinkle flour on sizzling fat, bursting the starch grains, and add liquid to make a smooth emulsion that slips down the throat. We pound and chop, beat and batter, whisk and fold, mixing ingredients, making magic. What stranger alchemy can there be than the transformation of the pale jelly of an egg white into a snowy cloud?

Add sugar *fine as the softest sand* and the mixture turns glossy. Heat it slowly and it solidifies into crispness as light as fluff. In its small way, a meringue is a miracle. So is mayonnaise, or caramel, a cake or a soufflé, a gin and tonic.

Cookery is full of minor miracles – concoctions that defy the inexperienced to guess at their ingredients, recipes that are the result of centuries of experiment and a thousand happy accidents. At its most expressive, cookery is an art that can ravish not only our mouths with taste and texture, but also our noses and eyes. Even, in extreme cases, our ears. In medieval courts and wealthy homes until the sixteenth century there was a fashion for what we might call 'novelty cuisine'.

Huge pies were baked blind, opened and filled with something unexpected, like a live snake. Song birds were particularly popular, hence the four and twenty blackbirds baked for the king, a culinary flourish to include the last of our five senses in the recipe.

Although our lips are disproportionately sensitive, alive to the minutest nuances of texture and temperature, our sense of taste is not especially sophisticated. Sprinkled over the tongue are ten thousand tiny projections, papillae, which carry the taste buds. Despite their number and acuity (we can discern bitterness at levels of one part in two million), taste buds only respond to four basic flavours: *sour, salt, bitter and sweet.* The tip of the tongue is particularly responsive to salt and sweet tastes, its sides recognise sour flavours, and the back of the tongue responds to bitter tastes. Beyond these fundamentals, the building blocks of all flavour, every other subtlety, the endless and wonderful variety that is the very spice of a fine meal, is perceived through our sense of smell. This is why eating becomes so much less pleasurable with a cold; without the information from our noses, ploughing through a meal can be as dull as munching cardboard.

Although diet and table manners vary widely in different cultures, some customs and preferences which hark back to man's early history are universal. A sweet tooth is a weakness we all share and seems to be the legacy of our herbivorous past. Fruit is at its *sweetest when perfectly ripe,* when also at its most nutritious. We are born with

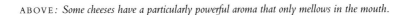

ABOVE: *Some cheeses have a particularly powerful aroma that only mellows in the mouth.*

LEFT: *Our tongues are peppered with taste buds, but they are only programmed to react to four basic tastes: salt, bitter, sour and sweet. Every other nuance and subtlety of flavour, the variety that is the very spice of our diet, is perceived through the olfactory membrane in our noses where the odour of what we are eating is diffused from our mouths. Without a sense of smell we would be unable to make a distinction in taste between honey, chocolate and sugar, or between a lemon and a lime, between salmon and monk fish, or between coffee and chicory.*

RIGHT: *Pasta is a perfect comfort food – simple, filling, homely. Bland in taste, it does have textural interest, cooked al dente in a myriad of shapes. A culinary blank canvas, it forms the basis of a thousand different dishes and flavours.*

this preference, perfectly catered for by human breast milk which is distinctly sweet, and carry it into adulthood. An addiction to anchovies is unheard of, yet self-confessed 'chocoholics' abound.

A sweet tooth is alien to the true carnivore but our predatory past has left its own mark, not only on what we eat but on how we choose to enjoy it. Our preference for eating as a communal activity, and for taking one, possibly two, large meals a day instead of continual snacking, harks back to the feasting after a kill. Although the timing of main meals, and even their number, has varied over history and according to culture, a principal meal, taken as a group, remains *central to our social lives* both within the family and beyond. Eating alone, without even a television or a book alongside as companion, remains an uncomfortable experience. Eating marks out both the shape of our days and the pattern of our lives; breakfast, lunch and dinner, birthdays, weddings and wakes. Whether paired or in a social group, food is the focus of some of the most important moments of our lives, the oil that frees-up the machinery, the substance of celebration.

As tiny babies and toddlers, food is one of the few areas of activity over which we can exert control. Refusal of food offered by a mother anxious to see her child well nourished is a power game indulged by all babies. According to modern psychology, feeding your child is an emotional minefield, and one that few negotiate without the odd small explosion. At its most simple, the offering of food is an act of love; its refusal, a rejection. No wonder as adults we binge on chocolate if

The scents of baking pastry and freshly ground coffee are a delicious rehearsal for the

pleasures of a continental breakfast. A steaming cappuccino, bitter coffee masked under

its layer of sweet foam, and a warm croissant – buttery dough inside a crisp and flaky

skin – a combination of tastes, textures and temperatures worth getting out of bed for.

LEFT: *Discovering tastes and textures that complement one another – here, fresh tuna, lime leaves and potato – is the essence of culinary creativity.*

CENTRE: *Salty parmesan, a vibrant foil for pasta or the juicy flesh of a ripe pear.*

RIGHT: *The crunch of firm apple, pure nutrition prettily packaged.*

lonely when, as children, a chocolate biscuit was produced from the tin for every grazed knee. No wonder we treat ourselves to a chocolate bar, feeling at once guilty and defiant, if sweets were only available as reward or celebration. Eating disorders are a sad and extreme reflection of what, at worst, can be a fraught relationship with food. Exacerbating the tensions are problems associated with body image and dieting – an obsession fed by the media's endless display of physical perfection in all its naked, and for most of us, unattainable glory.

While food is a fraught subject for an unhappy minority, and the subject of much debate, for most of us, it is *a voluptuous delight.* And not only in its consumption. Cookery, more than a chore, has become a leisure activity, the kitchen a grown-up playground. The kitchen has assumed a new role in the modern household. Far from the hidden domain of the past where servants slaved out of sight and mind, kitchens are now thought of as the very heart of the home. To achieve this in houses built to suit different attitudes, walls are knocked down, former reception rooms furnished with Agas and butler's sinks. Modern houses make kitchens central to their lay-out. This, rather than the dining room or drawing room, is where we entertain, its design as much to do with display as efficiency.

For centuries, people only cooked for themselves if they could not afford to pay someone else to do it for them. Even the most modest of nineteenth-century suburban households could employ a cook. Subsequently, the twentieth century has seen two major changes in the introduction of electricity and the disappearance of the servant class, which revolutionized the structure of society and of the home. When every kitchen task had to be done by hand, from fetching the water to lighting the fire, from laboriously turning the spit to beating the cream, cookery was hard, physical work, which was as tiring as it was time-consuming. Large households were serviced by a small army of workers from scullery maids to butlers who devoted much of their time to the provision of meals. Making a fruit cake, with its *grinding of spices* and beating of heavy ingredients, was more like a work-out at the gym than a creative way to relax.

The modern kitchen, however, is equipped with an array of labour-saving devices which now seem so ordinary we forget to appreciate them. Manufacturers predict that, among other gadgets, we will soon see voice-activated ovens which can assess the food put inside them and automatically select the cooking levels required.

Alongside this elevation of the kitchen from workhouse to status symbol has been the emergence of the chef as celebrity and, with it, an incredible proliferation of restaurants. Eating out is now one of our most popular entertainments, whether a burger and coke or the full artistry of Michelin-starred gastronomy. Only thirty years ago, the choice was likely to be limited to the cuisines of India or France. Now, in larger cities, there is scarcely a corner of the world not represented by cookery from Greece to Italy, Japan to Thailand, Arabia to South America, Spain to China.

The pleasure of eating in a restaurant or café is more than the sum of its menu, more than the satisfaction of a break with routine and the treat of being waited on. Furnishings, lighting, music, the paintings on the walls, the spacing and design of tables and chairs, the table linen, the cutlery and crockery, even the dress code of waiters and waitresses, all have an influence on our appreciation of the food we are served.

At home, all these elements are equally important and, moreover, within our control. From the furniture we choose for dining down to the salt and pepper and the flowers on the table, the way we serve our food makes an important difference to the way we enjoy it.

Probably the most simple, if seasonally dependent, way to turn a meal into an occasion is to eat it outdoors. The continental habit of scattering the pavements with tables and chairs is spreading, while barbecues, with their hearty air of boy-scout improvisation, scent summer evenings with the smoke of *a thousand sizzling sausages.* Picnics can be eaten anywhere and to any level of sophistication: on the beach, at the gymkhana or the races, watching the boating, or during the interval of an opera; any excuse and we pack our wicker hampers and spread our rugs.

Food has always been susceptible to fashion. Nutmeg was so chic in the seventeenth century that people carried their own supplies, complete with tiny graters. Recent food fads have been fast and furious; the 'revival' of black forest gâteau and prawn cocktail, those staples of the seventies' dinner party, has been greeted with the wonder that accompanies the discovery of a quaint antique. We read cookery books in bed, we watch cookery programmes on television, we are endlessly given new recipes in magazines and newspapers, on the backs of packets and the insides of lids. The restaurant critic has more status than those who opine on theatre or ballet. Never, it seems, have we been so obsessed with what we eat. But then, never has the quality and choice of our food been more irresistible.

RIGHT: *Crystal clear water, the essence of life; licking a chocolate-covered ice cream, simple indulgence.*

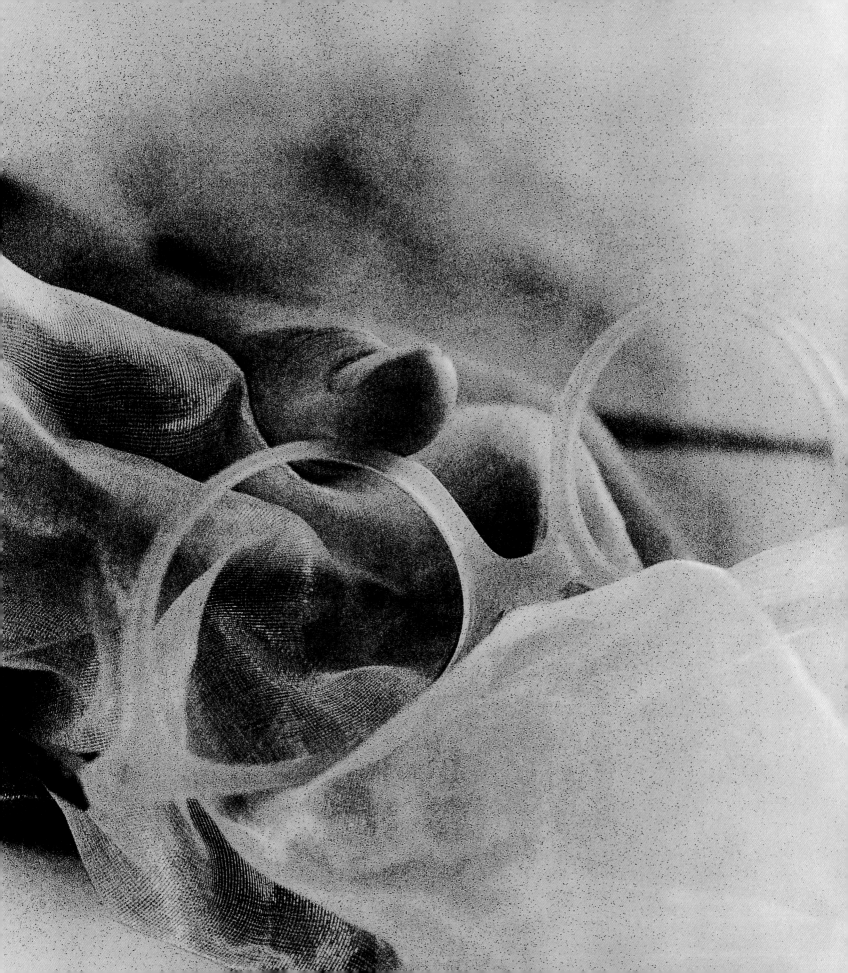

SIGHT

A certain colour tones you up.

MATISSE

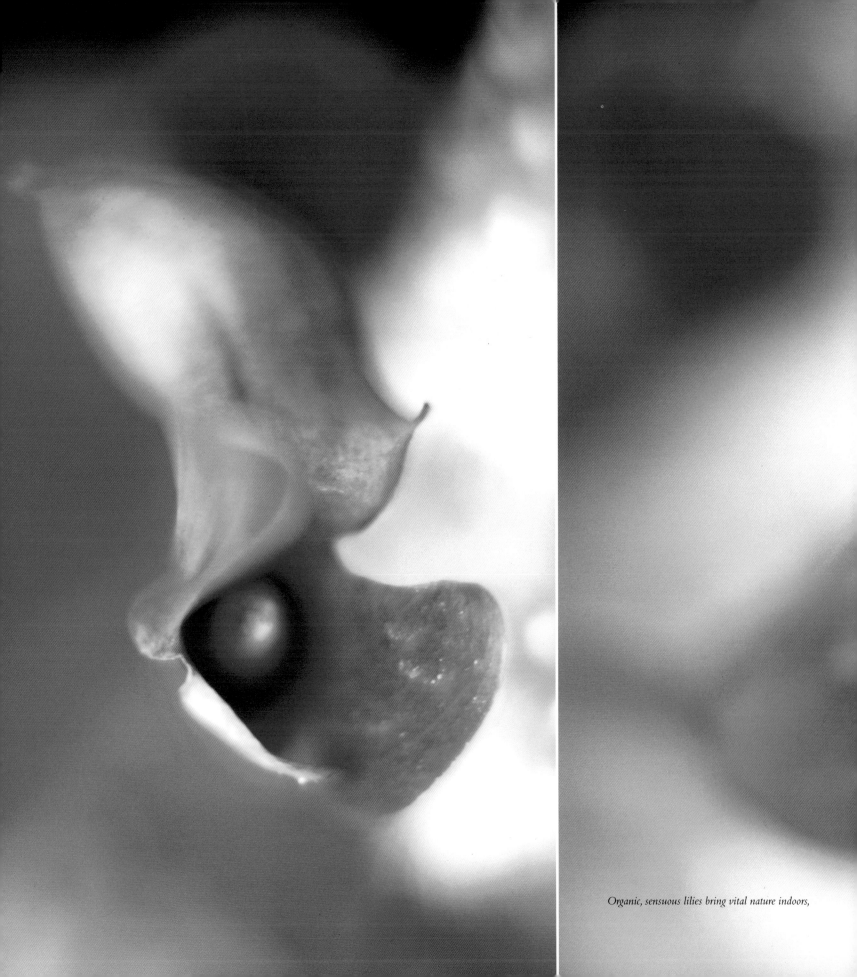

Organic, sensuous lilies bring vital nature indoors,

colour and shape combining to make living decoration in man-made spaces.

Of all our senses, sight is the most precious, the most dominating in the hierarchy of perception. Through our eyes, we appreciate beauty, recognize the familiar, and recoil from danger. Our eyes are hungry for information and hunters of pleasure. When we fall in love, we gaze at the face of our beloved with devouring intensity. When we stand before a painting we adore, our eyes drink it in. Beauty is sustenance for our souls. And, despite nature's abundant provision of it, human beings have an abiding need to make their own, from the cave paintings of Lescaux, to the Sistine Chapel, to Disneyland.

Highly sensitive, the human eye can discern differences between several million colours of varying hue and can detect the presence of light equivalent to one candle at a distance of ten miles. So important and so delicate is the surface of the eye that it is protected from injury by *an endless bathing of tears* and sweeping of blinks, fringed by dust-catching lashes, hooded by the shutters of our eye-lids. These are our windows onto the world, a planet ablaze with colour.

To deprive someone of light, or sight, is one of the cruellest tortures. Medieval dungeons were not windowless for reasons of security alone. Even in our more, literally, enlightened times, a prison cell with a picture window would not seem a suitable place of punishment, however thick the plexiglass and hefty the bars. Victorians wept at the pathos of Millais' *The Blind Girl* who feels the grass between her fingers but cannot see the double rainbow, the birds, the flowers, or the butterfly that has landed, unnoticed, on her shawl.

Inside our own homes, on our own territory, we can choose to give our eyes pleasure. Everyone has suffered the discomfort of a room – perhaps a waiting-room at the dentist – where there is nothing of interest, distinction or charm upon which to rest the gaze; eyes wander disconsolately from scuffed carpet the colour of dung, over walls of lumpy porridge, to a yellowing ceiling of sickening swirls of textured paint. Chairs are chipped dark varnish and stained orange weave, and there is a poster on the wall showing a diagram of tooth decay and a photograph of bleeding gums. The view from the window, which might have shown a patch of sky or scrap of foliage, is veiled in white polyester bobbled by use and grey at the edges. After about five minutes the visual deprivation starts to bite. The world begins to seem dreary, joyless. No wonder the mind dwells on whining drills and long needles. At the other end of the visual scale are rooms and spaces created to dazzle and amaze – magnificent, overwhelming interiors like the Salle des Glaces at Versailles; rooms of swooning beauty like the Heaven

Room at Burghley House with its ceiling of voluptuous nudes; of breath-taking visual trickery like Rex Whistler's trompe l'oeil drapery at Port Lympne; of extraordinary skill like the Grinlin Gibbons' carvings that seem to grow out of the panelling in rooms at Hampton Court. If the dentist's waiting-room represents famine, these rooms equate to twenty-course banquets.

Most of us are more comfortable with something in between. Visual pleasure, as all dentists should remember, need be neither expensive nor opulent. Too much richness is indigestible. Eyes are equally satisfied with less sophisticated treats: a row of favourite postcards, *sunlight slanting across a white wall*, a branch of lilac in a milk bottle, a cotton sheet, starched and ironed. Marie-Antoinette herself sought escape from the over-powering grandeur of the palace in her more simply decorated private apartments and in the faux rustic simplicity of the Petit Hameau.

'Let there be light' said God, and only then did He wrap the world with oceans and mountains, and people it with animals and man. The Biblical metaphor has stood the test of science. Light is life in the most literal sense – without it the simplest plant-life cannot photosynthesize.

From earliest times, mankind has worshipped the sun, recognizing its life-giving force. Ever since architecture became an art as much as a necessity, we have played with its visual effects. Even before the availability of window glass, the rich chose to retire to a room separated from the medieval great hall, lit by huge windows and called the 'solar', or sun room. As the only window-coverings in thirteenth-century Europe were shutters, and sometimes oiled paper, or horn, presumably the amount of sunshine admitted was entirely seasonal.

A room that is flooded with sunlight is a room full of life. We can maximize its intensity by reflecting it in light colours, redoubling its brightness with mirrors or polished metal. But we also need to control it, shade ourselves from its heat, soften and diffuse its glare.

Ideally, a room will be flexible enough to make the most of light when it is weak, and form a shield when it is strong. Venetian blinds and louvred shutters slice sunlight into slanting shadows; muslin curtains muffle and mute it; frosted glass dilutes it. *Control is key*. Like shade on a beach, a means of filtering excess light is essential. While sunlight may beautify a room, it can also destroy its contents. Antique textiles, fine woods and inlays, paintings, drawings, even photographs, all decay when exposed to too much sunlight.

Shutters form an architectural screen, controlling the intensity of daylight, providing privacy, their formal lines broken by the modest curves of hull and sail.

RIGHT: *Groupings of objects make an arresting focus; the boisterous yellow glaze of a bottle emphasizes the oddity of its form, a man-made concentrate next to nature's own colours and curves.*

OVERLEAF LEFT: *Cool monochromes, like a black and white film, draw attention to form.*

OVERLEAF RIGHT: *Sunlight throws the swoops of an antique sofa into a strong relief of light and shade and gives sinuous lilies a translucent glow.*

White paint opens space, reflecting light and
redoubling its intensity. Mirrors magnify the effect,
gathering brightness like magnets and bouncing it
back into a room, their reflections offering an illusion
of another world beyond the wall.

RIGHT: *Shades of white, its brilliance subtly altered
by form and texture.*

Over-exposure is to be avoided, but natural light – a mixture of direct sunlight and reflected sky light – is the light we all prefer to live and work under. Globally and locally according to season, the suicide rate reflects the intensity and duration of sunlight available. The smaller the doses of sunlight, the greater the likelihood of depression.

Artists have always chosen to work illuminated by a north light, under which colours are shown at their most 'true'. One of many contributors to the relatively recent phenomenon of 'office sickness' appears to be the effect of cheap fluorescent lighting – a flat, cold, bright, unflattering light that casts few shadows and no highlights. Research indicates that proximity to *natural light* in an office increases both efficiency and a sense of well-being. Full-spectrum artificial lighting, the closest we can get to imitation sunlight, is increasingly recognized as a sound investment, whether to illuminate the factory floor or the indoor pool.

While windows are an essential, a view is an added extra. A green landscape, mountains and water, gardens and beach, probably come at the top of the list, but even a vista of chimney pots and television aerials, or *a sky-light framing the clouds*, have the charm of leading our focus past the walls and into the distance. A view gives a room a sense of place; it can entice us out or make us glad to be indoors. To prevent the world looking back in, or to hide a view we would rather not see, we can screen our windows – but at the expense of that added dimension seen through glass, the world beyond.

Glass, like electricity, is a modern luxury. Until the mid-nineteenth century, window glass was only available in sheets so limited that in order to construct a window of any size, many panes had to be held together. The history of fenestration graphically reflects the advances in sheet glass technology, from the tiny leaded diamond panes of the fifteenth and sixteenth centuries, through the multi-paned Georgian sash window, to the suburban bays of late Victorian terraced houses divided into eight large panes of glass.

Today we can build a house completely of glass. If anything will distinguish the domestic buildings of the twentieth century, it will be the size and number of windows: glass ceilings, atria, domes, and pyramids, all designed to fill our indoor spaces with sky and sunlight. The exceptions are the proliferation of ersatz period houses that now fringe so many villages. These invariably interpret the vernacular by imitating the small windows that were once a necessity for all but the wealthy. It seems a strange sacrifice for the sake of a stylistic gesture towards a less-privileged past. The compromise has been the conservatory. Its popularity – bursting out of the rear façade of practically every other house that appears in style magazines – is symptomatic of our craving for indoor sunlight and delight in breaking down the barriers between the outdoor and indoors.

When the sun sinks and night falls we are faced with a choice of illumination that would have fascinated our fire-lit ancestors. Like glass, an effective means of artificial light was terribly expensive before the nineteenth century. Beeswax candles were the Rolls Royce of lighting; chandeliers that were designed to hold them by the dozen were an *outrageous extravagance*. For most people, a smelly, sputtering, dimly burning rush dipped in fat was the only supplement to firelight. Consequently, most people went to bed when it got dark, and rose when it became light.

Nowadays, we are spoilt for choice with our permanent supply of electricity, our cheap and effective tungsten filament or low-voltage halogen bulbs, our dimmer switches and spotlights. So spoilt, in fact, that we even call in specialist lighting designers who will up-light or down-light our walls, wash our floors or ceilings with light, pin-point a sculpture, turn our rooms into theatres of light that will change in mood at the press of a button. Even without the help of experts, good lighting is so readily available – table lamps, standard lamps, recessed spots, wall lights – there can never again be an excuse for the blank, ugly monotony of the single central ceiling light that shows up the bags under our eyes and the sags in our upholstery with cruel precision.

Despite all this technology we return to candles for special occasions; we blow them out on birthday cakes, we light them in our churches, we sit round them for an expensive or intimate meal. Candlelight is not a good light by which to read, or sew, or work, but its warm yellow cast makes skin look smooth and peachy and its *gentle glow and hazy shadows* flatter a dark room better than any other light. Not to have the choice, of course, is plain irritating. A blown fuse or a power cut inevitably results in an evening of furious fumbling. But, with the power of electricity at our fingertips, a bath by candlelight or a conversation by firelight is as soothing as a mother's lullaby.

Newton was the first to discover that sunlight is composed of the colours of the spectrum. Colour is light and everything we see is distinguished by the way light reflects from it. Iridescent colours are caused when white light reflects off a surface – a soap bubble, a film of oil, *a dragonfly's wing* – the structure of which disperses the light into its component colours. Most animals and plants owe their colours to pigments which absorb certain wave-lengths from the light and reflect others back to the eye. The rainbow, one of the sky's most ravishing displays, and the subject of endless myth and legend, is a glorious demonstration of Newton's discovery.

Most of the colour that surrounds us is beyond our control: the blues of the sky, the browns of the earth, the greens of the grass, the dead grey of tarmac. But inside our homes and outside in our gardens we can tame and imitate nature, reflect or reject its million hues.

Artists instinctively use colour to express mood. 'A certain blue enters your soul. A certain red has an effect on your blood pressure', wrote Matisse. In Munch's account of his highly-charged painting *The Scream* he describes how he 'painted the clouds as red blood – the colours were screaming'. Kandinsky was also convinced of the power of colour, and again invokes the soul as most sensitive to its mastery. 'Colour directly influences the soul. Colour is the keyboard, the eyes are the hammers, the soul is the piano with many strings.' And, although science has yet to provide conclusive proof of the emotional and psychological *effects of colour*, we all know from simple experience that its messages to the brain can be potent.

Some 'rules' relating to colour have gained consensus. Based on the colour wheel which puts the three primaries, blue, red and yellow, at equal distances and fills in the gaps with the secondary colours mixed from them, and tertiary colours mixed from the secondaries, some simple observations can be made. Colours on the blue and green side of the wheel are called 'cool' and 'receding', colours on the red and orange side 'warm' and 'advancing'. The cooler side of the wheel is said to include the colours that are most serene – hence, presumably, the frequent use of a nasty pale green in hospitals (the brighter green of operating gowns and sheets is an attempt to minimize the optical after-effect of long focusing on the colour red), and the back-stage 'green rooms' of television studios and theatres traditionally used to keep guests and actors calm. On the other side of the wheel, red and orange are often cited as invigorating, energetic colours. Colours opposing one another on the wheel are 'complementary' and are often used by artists to create striking effects. The Impressionists, some of whom studiously avoided the use of black, preferred to use a colour's *complementary shade* to darken it. The technique can equally be applied to mixing paints for decorating and has subtle results.

Even hugely expanded, the colour wheel only shows one dimension of colour, known as its 'hue'. But there are many hundreds of different colours we might call red, just as there are many hundreds of greens in a forest; there are delicious pinks and hideous ones. A room painted a deep, dark red can be as comforting as a hot water bottle; the same room in a bright, shiny, poppy red feels fraught, agitated. A wall of glowing, buttercup yellow is like concentrated sunshine. But a yellow with a tinge of green may appear nauseating, which is why yellow is avoided for aeroplane interiors. These endless variations are due to the fact that colour has two further dimensions, 'saturation', which describes the vividness of a hue, and 'lightness', which refers to the amount of white or black mixed in with it.

At the very furthest ends of the colour spectrum are those potently symbolic opposites, black and white, representing maximum darkness and lightness; night and day; evil and good; death and birth. Different cultures have varied in their interpretations of these antagonists, the beginning and the end of colour. In Western cultures, white signifies *purity and innocence*, but in Japan a bride wears white at her wedding to symbolize her death to her family. For Hindus, white is the colour of the Brahmin, the highest caste. Islamic women wear black as a sign of religious conformity and obedience. In the West, it is the colour of melancholy and mourning, and also of the smartest little dresses.

Our emotional reaction to colour is both complex and ultimately personal. We all have our own associations and particular favourites. And the colours we like to wear may be very different from the ones that we choose for our walls, floors and cushions. Context is vital to our appreciation of colour. The *jumble of shades* that we call beautiful in a traditional cottage garden border might appal in a kitchen. The radiance of a summer sky is vulgar in a suit. The subtle green of an avocado loses its charm as a lavatory seat.

White is light and, in its purest form, also an absence of colour. White paint can disguise ugly proportions or show off fine ones, flatter the wobbly walls of a cottage or emphasize the pristine planes of a newly plastered loft conversion. The enduring popularity of white has provoked some to condemn it as boring. 'Magnolia', a perfectly pleasant shade of off-white, has long been a by-word for boring, suburban non-taste. But, for those who love light, and even, perversely, colour, white can prove to be an irresistible choice. White will frame any other shade, bright or subtle, without fighting it.

White paint has slipped in and out of fashion since the early eighteenth century when the craze for Palladian architecture made pale stone or plaster the most desirable interior finish. While impoverished cottagers continued, as always, to whitewash or limewash their walls, the owners of grander homes heightened the effects of classical splendour with liberal use of white, pearl and stone.

Not only was white a fashionable colour, later adopted as a foil for the gilded dancing *curlicues of rococo*, it was also less expensive than brighter colours, all of which contained costly pigments. When made with white lead it had the added advantage of acting as a preservative. Less noxious was distemper, made from ground chalk mixed with size made from boiled animal skins and horns, while limewash, used on rendered walls or plaster, was made from lime putty.

All these types of paint had their disadvantages. White lead mixed with linseed oil discoloured, while distemper and limewash rubbed off. Gradually, techniques for producing longer-lasting, less fugitive whites improved. But even in the increasingly industrialized Victorian era, when cheap wallpapers largely usurped the role of paint, colours faded and decayed. The mass-produced, cheap and effective household paints we now take for granted are a relatively recent phenomenon.

Throughout this century, white has been the best-selling paint colour. The Edwardians created pretty, feminine interiors with furniture, as well as walls and ceilings painted white. At the Paris exhibition in 1925, which gave its name to the style Art Deco, Le Corbusier announced the modernist agenda with his white cube pavilion and its proto-minimalist interior. Dubbed by one contemporary critic 'the cold storage warehouse cube', it had mostly white walls and was considered sterile and ugly. With hindsight it looks seminal. Certainly its yellow filing cabinets and bentwood chairs would look perfectly at home in a fin de siècle Habitat catalogue. White has remained the choice of the modernist architect and decorator the essence of minimal decoration, classless and timeless, clean and cool.

White also became the calling-card of a less uncompromising modern style. Decorator Syrie Maugham's all-white drawing-room of 1930 proved just as influential as Le Corbusier's 'machine for living', and was far more comfortable. In a palette of soft and off-whites with *richly textured* cream rugs, low beige satin sofas and an etiolated screen of mirror and chrome it was much photographed and admired at the time. Nearly seventy years later it lives on, unwittingly plagiarized in endless penthouses and duplexes the wealthy world over.

Just as Le Corbusier set the scene for modernism with his white cube pavilion, Syrie Maugham and her American contemporary Elsie de Woolf set the seal on white, and *shades of white*, as the palette of expensive, modern chic. The associations have stuck. Like the freshly laundered shirt of the banker, the crisp linen sheets of the most exclusive hotels, the fluffy white towels of the luxury gym, white walls, white curtains, white upholstery and pale rugs spell high-maintenance and money as well as good looks.

Go to any paint shop today and you will be presented with a bewildering array of shades of white – a hint of apricot, a *soupçon* of bluebell, a touch of butter. John Fowler, the great country house decorator, used white softened with a little raw umber, a warm white with a look of venerable ageing. Today's brilliant whites generally incorporate a tinge of blue, which, while emphasizing that clean dazzle so beloved of washing powder makers, can be cold in a room.

Colour can transform a space more effectively than any other form of decoration. Paint a room forest green, or royal blue, or plum red, and it will draw in its walls around you. Paint the same room white and there is *an instant illusion of space*. White ceilings rise up, white floors bounce back so much light they seem to float. Even a basement room with minimal natural light can be brightened beyond recognition with a coat of white paint.

Light and colour are the basics of any interior, but form, space and pattern have an equally essential role in the creation of architectural beauty. Like colour, often used to adjust our perception of space in a room, volume, or the lack of it, can elicit an emotional response.

Broadly speaking, high ceilings and empty expanses of floor have an uplifting effect. It is impossible to enter the lofty vaulting of Kings College Chapel in Cambridge, or stand beneath the soaring dome of Hagia Sophia in Istanbul without experiencing a rush of awe and excitement. The scale of these buildings is neither available, nor appropriate for domestic use. But the conversion of warehouses and old factories, and redundant Victorian institutional buildings like schools and asylums, has provided a new source of homes which can satisfy for some the craving for space, even if it is at the expense of multiple bedrooms. Going open-plan, knocking down walls, opening up staircases, produces a new sense of flow in any house. Even the most modest two bedroom semi can appear spacious given the discipline of all white paint, a single floor covering throughout, and minimal furnishing.

RIGHT: *An arrangement which invites the eye to make distinctions. Cushions and upholstery reflect colours and corners from the painting above, both softened and mediated by texture and the way it reflects light, and by the contrast between one-dimensional representation and three-dimensional comfort.*

Low ceilings and busy furnishings are, at worst claustrophobic, at best cosy. A total lack of cosiness in a house is almost as hard to bear as rampant clutter. Even the most hardened loft-liver needs a corner to retreat to sometimes, a place that feels *enclosed and private*. It could simply be an over-sized armchair with a favourite cushion.

Straight lines characterize the shell of most buildings, but the eye is easily bored by the sight of nothing but angles and hard edges; it seeks relief in curves and soft lines and is excited by the interplay of the two. Hogarth writing in the eighteenth century proposed that a *'serpentine line of beauty'* was present in all things thought to be beautiful. And the suggestion has often been made that we find curves pleasing for their affinity with the rounded lines of our own bodies which we are, quite naturally, programmed to find attractive.

Similarly, the tension between symmetry and asymmetry is visually stimulating. Analysis of the way we look at a painting has revealed what is called a 'glance curve', a typical way of scanning an image that tracks from the bottom left-hand side and upwards towards the right. Long before psychologists charted this phenomenon, artists were instinctively using this pattern of looking in the composition of their paintings by favouring an asymmetrical arrangement which leads the eye through the narrative of a painting towards the top right-hand side of the image. The very fact that the majority of us are, and always have been, right-handed is indicative of the brain's natural bias towards asymmetry, a bias linked to the difference in the ways the two cerebral hemispheres function.

Perfect symmetry, like straight lines, is usually seen as a human imposition of order on the chaos of the natural world. Pascal posited that our taste for symmetry is derived from the human face, 'Hence we demand symmetry horizontally and in breadth only'. Certainly, the *interplay between symmetry* and its opposite attracts and interests us, as do any visual tensions between the plain and the patterned, the busy and the simple.

Contrast is as appealing to the eye as it is to the stomach, the spice that gives the recipe its bite. An interior that consists entirely of straight lines is brought to life by a spiral staircase; *a riot of rococo curlicues* is thrown into relief by the geometry of a chequerboard floor; a diet of unrelieved clutter is as irksome as a blank cell is numbing.

Any interior can play with these contrasts to provide surprise and interest. A cluster of objects in a room that is otherwise spare introduces a change of tempo; several clusters and you have a rhythm. The surprise might be a splash of colour in a sea of neutral tones or a vase of rampant

Colour is visual pleasure. LEFT: *A vase of flowers with all the impact of a painting.*

RIGHT: *A pile of resin plates, soap on a dish – splashes of brightness.*

FAR LEFT: *Fire has lost none of its fascination in an age of technology. Flickering like a liquid mobile made of light, blazing logs make the most alluring of all visual foci, seducing and entertaining the eye with infinitely suggestive shapes and shadows, their warmth comforting, their light flattering.*

LEFT: *Tools as ornament – a simple wooden pot of long matches makes the useful attractive.*

roses in a clinical, white-tiled bathroom. Or the shock of the new could result from a change of mood between rooms and spaces, the difference between inside and outside.

Clever, thoughtful and unusual placings of objects and furnishings can elevate the ordinary to the interesting just as a good frame can make a mediocre picture look like art. The selection of those objects and furnishings, as opposed to their arrangement, the colours of our walls or the drape of our curtains, is probably the most intimate reflection of our tastes and preferences. All are subject to the *vagaries of fashion*. The 'density', as Peter Thornton calls it, of objects in rooms is one very obvious cycle. More recently advertisements for Swedish furnishings superstore IKEA have encouraged the stylish, young home-owner to 'chuck out the chintz'; the very chintz that was at the apogee of interior fashion in the 1980s when everyone wanted their drawing-room to look like a version of a grand English rectory with saggy sofas, pleated silk lamp shades and woolwork cushions galore.

Within the often unconsciously felt constraints of fashion, our homes remain the largest stage for the display of our individualism. Homes are an outer clothing, 'our larger body', and the way we fill and decorate them is a means of saying something about our aspirations, our personal histories, our interests, values and self-perceptions via a series of complicated and sophisticated signals. Even the very wealthy who call in an interior decorator to design everything for them down to the colour and shape of the bathroom soap are revealing something personal. Their choice of decorator, whether cutting-edge modern or establishment traditional, carries a message in itself, while the handing over to a professional of an activity that is usually private makes the point that they are too busy with more important business than nest-building and also rich enough to afford an expensive and indulgent service which most people naturally undertake themselves.

For those of us who enjoy the process of feathering our nests there are many reasons why we choose the things that fill it. Some are not chosen; they are made by our children, or given to us by friends, or inherited from family. Others, however, are chosen as souvenirs, or because they are useful or functional. Some are chosen simply because we find them beautiful. Each person will feel comfortable with a different proportion of the above – from those who will happily banish anything that they do not find aesthetically pleasing, whatever its sentimental value, to those who will find a room frighteningly sterile if it isn't stuffed with things of emotional resonance.

In the nineteenth century, William Morris, that great idealist and aesthete, famously argued that we should have nothing in our homes that was not either useful or beautiful. Morris would be amazed at the number of 'useful' items a modern home is expected to accommodate; refrigerators, microwaves, kettles, computers, stereos, televisions, fax and answering machines. Much ingenuity has been expended on ways to hide and disguise these useful things whether as elaborate Sheraton cupboards, or behind the doors of a stately-home dairy. More recently, the trend has been to make the useful thing itself more attractive – radiators have blossomed into conversation pieces and cookers have put on armour of brushed stainless steel panels and nickel-plated knobs.

Beauty is at once obvious and elusive, personal and collective. When Morris talked of 'beauty' in a domestic context, he referred to the hand-crafted, faintly rustic designs of which he himself approved. Great philosophers have struggled to find definitions that will tie beauty down, and failed. While there are many points of convergence – it would be hard to find someone who did not *find beauty in a flower*, or a sunset – there are just as many points of divergence. Contemporary art is a morass of divergences as experts and scholars and connoisseurs and laymen battle out the merits of piles of bricks and half cows where some find beauty (and meaning) and others don't.

Some predilections can be short-lived. Our grandchildren will consider pierced navels as unattractive as today's teenagers think them erotic. Interior decoration has a slower cycle of fashion but is just as susceptible. But some *species of beauty* have a constant appeal. While changing tastes in body shapes have variously required cod-pieces, farthingales, corsets and degrees of fatness and thinness, a clear skin has always been a *sine qua non* of physical beauty. The classical orders of architecture, founded by the Greeks, have inspired buildings generally thought beautiful for thousands of years. For reasons that remain mysterious, we find their proportions endlessly pleasing.

The painter Constable asserted that he 'never saw anything ugly … for let the form of an object be what it may – light, shade, and perspective will always make it beautiful'. Admittedly, Constable died too long ago to witness the stained concrete and pebble-dash that characterize our nastier multi-storey car parks, but perhaps even a car park painted by Constable might acquire a certain romance. In the end, the old cliché of beauty resting in the eye of the beholder may be our best stab at a definitive statement. Giving our own eyes the kind of beauty they most appreciate is what we aim for in our homes.

RIGHT: *A plain, black pot, pierced with minimal decoration provides rich food for visual digestion; texture is suggested by the play of light on smooth glaze; contrast is at maximum stretch between darkness and lightness; geometric shapes are subtly modified by the irregularity of the hand-made - the most simple ingredients, a visual feast.*

SOUND

Music, when soft voices die
Vibrates in the memory

BYRON

The moon is a completely silent place. Once, when the heavy boots of astronauts scuffed its dust, there was a muffled tremor of footsteps, but they were only as loud as the vibrations of the moon rock itself and nobody heard them. Encased in their moon suits, the astronauts communicated by radio. Without a medium such as air, without all those millions of molecules shaking backwards and forwards, there is no such thing as noise. If we lived in a vacuum, there would be no howling car alarms, no sonic boom, no songs, no music. We may curse the sounds that disturb us, but if we lived on the soundless moon, there is much more we would miss: *the noise of life*. Even before we are born we are listening, lulled by the incessant boom of our mother's heart-beat, faster at times of fear and excitement, slow and steady in sleep.

Sound is energy – a movement of air that we detect with our ears and hear with our brain. The vibrations that produce sound are carried in waves. When the waves strike our tiny ear-drums, the smallest three bones in our body are rocked into action, causing the fluid in the snail coil of our inner ear to move and to disturb microscopic hairs that line it, sending messages of infinite subtlety to our brains.

Part of this subtlety is in the brain's judicious selection of which noises to take note of and which to ignore. In our early days as hunters and predators this must have been an essential tool; the ability to ignore the rustle of the wind in order to concentrate on the crackle of hoof on twig. And equally useful defensively when listening for the sounds of pursuit. Unexpected noise makes us jump, sending adrenaline coursing more instantly than an alarm signal from any other of our senses. To lie awake at night rigid with tension, at the mercy of an unexplained sound, however tiny, is to be back in the dark jungle crouched in terror at the approach of some unknown danger.

In the modern urban jungle, the same unconscious aural filtering allows us to live with relatively high levels of background noise. The *distant purr* of a motorway or the nearby growl of urban traffic are screened out once registered as familiar and unthreatening, as is the ticking of an alarm clock. New noises, or noises that hold meaning for us, take precedence over the customary or continuous.

Sound selection also allows us, for example, to concentrate on one conversation in a room full of party chatter. A more dramatic instance of this process at work is the way in which a sleeping mother will be instantly woken by the cry of her baby, even when the sound of the cry is much quieter than the snores next to her ear. And, back at the noisy cocktail party, while concentrating on that one conversation amidst so many others, you may suddenly hear your name spoken on the other side of the room. The part of your hearing brain that is constantly listening, like a radioham, for significant noises has picked up the sound and pushed it forward into your consciousness.

Our perception of sound is a far more complicated process than we might at first appreciate. Many of our preferences and dislikes are entirely personal, music and musical tastes being the most obvious example. Culture and age have a part to play. The insistent electronic beat that sets teenage hearts racing, feet tapping with the urge to get up and dance, can cause sensations verging on the painful for their grandparents. Chinese music uses a different harmonic scale that may sound strange and whining to a Western ear.

But there are also all those sounds that inspire in us a whole range of positive emotions. Nature provides us with her own symphony. For millions of years before the chatter of human voices in conversation or song, the world was *humming with sound*: wind, ice, water, thunder, the hiss and bellow of violent eruptions, the whisper of reeds stirred by the current. Added to this was the cacophony of animal noise, from the grumble of the lion to the whirr of cicadas and the plaintive whistle of the whale.

Of all nature's instruments, the one of most abiding and universal appeal is water. Whether *the gentle applause of rain* on a glass roof or the rush of river over rock, the sound of water holds us in its thrall. Throughout history, pumps and gravity have been used in the great gardens of the world to create waterfalls and fountains. The lapping of tides on a sandy beach or the boom of waves against rock are two of the great joys of a house by the sea.

Indoor noises are mostly man-made. Some are so quiet or so habitual we hardly hear them. Some, like the telephone, the door bell or the alarm, are designed to attract attention. Most are so much a part of the fabric of domestic life we don't even think about whether we enjoy them or not; the sounds of cooking, the sounds of bathing, the sounds of domestic machinery from the quiet rumble of the tumble drier to the toy-town ping of the microwave. Making a list of favourite sounds is an interesting exercise; the *voices of people we love*, the throaty pop of a cork leaving a bottle, the controlled clang of a toaster, the clunk of a well-built car door, the rustle of a silk dress, the rattle of ice in a glass, the tiny tapping of a wrist watch. Life is full of good sounds that are taken for granted.

LEFT: *Sound can be torture or balm. Loud, sudden, or irregular noise tends to characterize the former. At the other end of the aural scale, the quiet, steady thrum of a fan is as calming as the breeze it creates is refreshing – a background frequency that soon becomes so familiar, it is forgotten.*

Affecting the timbre of all these sounds are the underlying acoustics of our homes. Bad acoustics can spoil the atmosphere of the most beautiful interior, making a room seem uncomfortable, unwelcoming and cold. The basic rules are simple; hard surfaces reflect sound waves, soft ones absorb them. The sound of voices in an empty room with a bare floor, as anyone who has moved into a house shorn of carpets and curtains knows, has an unpleasant echo.

In modern minimalist interiors with their characteristically hard floors, smooth surfaces and sparse use of fabrics, the acoustics, if not attended to, may be too 'lively'; footsteps ring, the clatter of crockery is amplified and the stereo resonates. This is a quality of sound we associate with public places like the empty lino strips of dreary institutional corridors. Architects sensitive to the impact of acoustics will frequently find ways to counteract too much reverberation without sacrificing good looks – *stretched fabric*, for example, can achieve the pared down simplicity of plain plaster without its sound-reflecting qualities; metal can be minutely perforated to encourage absorption, ceilings can be lined, or subtle texture introduced. Fitted carpet in small areas works wonders.

The level of people's tolerance to sound and noise depends very much on context and familiarity. People who move to the country to escape the urban hubbub are aggravated by the early morning dawn chorus, or the buzz of crop spraying, or the *village church bells*. Similarly, the same sound in different situations can evoke opposing responses. The music you choose for a party would be inappropriate at a funeral. You can shout on a football pitch but raised voices sound hysterical on a bowling green.

When it comes to unwelcome noise, control, or the lack of it, plays an important role in determining our reaction. Research has shown that people are least tolerant of noises that they believe are coming from 'next door', they are more accepting of noises from 'outside', and the most tolerant of noises from within their own household. Noise that is inflicted by a stranger is an invasion of territory which cannot be counteracted short of wearing ear-plugs or moving away from it and thereby relinquishing one's own territory.

In public places, we are at the mercy of sounds made by others, whether they be gunfire bursts of a pneumatic drill or the insistent tinnitus of a fellow passenger's personal stereo. At home, we can more easily be master of the sounds around us, although we cannot necessarily protect ourselves from unwanted noise as *effective sound-proofing* is not always practical. After the disastrous fire at Hampton Court Palace, the floor cavities were found to be filled with hundreds of thousands of crushed shells, an effective early means of deadening sound between floors. Modern architects are more likely to use fibre-glass wadding and, given the opportunity to start from scratch, have become adept at thorough sound-proofing, which remains problematic in an eighteenth-century terraced house. Thick curtains and shutters are aesthetically more acceptable than double-glazing, but typically thin party walls are less easy to deal with. Developing good relations with the neighbours is likely to be the best protection. In Japan, where houses were close together and also flimsily built, partly because of earthquakes, it became the custom to engage in particular domestic activities at particular times. Getting up, eating and then going to bed in unison was a way of minimizing the annoyance of noises from next door.

Of all the sounds that delight us, however, music remains the most powerful. Dance and rhythm, which are music's beginnings, are so natural, they are almost an instinct. Such is the strength of our attachment to rhythm that we are infected by it, whether we want to be or not. Just as we automatically *whistle a tune* in time with the beat of our feet on the pavement, so we are impelled to clean our teeth in time to the music on the radio.

Sounds generated by regular vibrations are those we generally term musical. Over the centuries we have defined and refined these sounds, and have invented a wide variety of ways of making them, to create a *language of incredible complexity*. Rules have been developed that govern rhythm with a discipline that ties it to time. Other rules, which vary between cultures, dictate pitch according to specific frequencies. Yet music remains the most mysterious of all art forms. A Brahms symphony uses sounds made by a range of means.

ABOVE: *The language of sound is not only confined to words and music. Our lives and our homes are full of sounds that carry meanings both general and specific; the soft, steady tick of a watch whose hands make their inexorable, circular journey through time, marks out the passing of the day with a whispered rhythm at once relentless and reassuring.*

The purposeful clang of a toaster is another kind of signal altogether,

a message that time is up and the task finished.

If random noise can affect us emotionally, how much more powerful is the effect of organized sound? Music is a mysterious master of mood control. In this house, speakers have been fitted into ceilings in every room, including bathrooms, allowing music to envelope the listener while its source remains discreet.

These include drawing roughened horse-hair across tightened cat gut, vibrating a sliver of reed with puffs of breath, and blowing raspberries into metal tubes, brings together many, many different types of musical sound. It turns them into a single musical entity with melodies and rhythms that can inspire us to skip or weep in turn.

Our bodies and our emotions are affected by music and not only by its rhythms but by its tempo and volume, its key and complexity. The precise mechanisms by which this musical language operates on our brains are still barely understood, but nevertheless its potency has been harnessed for thousands of years for rites and celebrations, for worship and mourning, for meditation and rabble-rousing from Gregorian chants to Zulu rain dances.

Most people's experience of music in the second half of the twentieth century has been dominated by the popular culture. While arguably 'pop' is a more simplistic genre than the music we call classical, we are nevertheless affected by it in ways we do not always recognize. Research by the Automobile Association in Britain has revealed that up-tempo rock music played loudly on the car stereo tends to increase a driver's speed and aggression.

Given the strength of its subliminal messages it really should come as no surprise that music has been hi-jacked by the marketing man. *Music can affect both behaviour and attitudes.* Restaurants and shops use it to encourage their customers to linger or to hurry them on to the check-out. The music that they choose will not only have an appropriate tempo, it will also be designed to appeal to a particular social type, thereby giving the product an especially attractive trademark or character.

At home we can manipulate our own moods with music, whether to intensify and enhance a particular emotion or to work against a feeling we want to shake off. Instead of leaving the radio burbling in the background, making a conscious decision to select a particular piece of music to bath, eat breakfast by or simply sit and listen to, can have an almost miraculous effects.

But this is the utilitarian approach of the salesman again. Music is far more than mood control. At its finest, it is pure pleasure. It is the most eternal of all our art forms, purely abstract. And because the meaning of music is felt, not understood, it seems to have something of the divine, a spiritual dimension that speaks to a part of us that has no other voice. A world without music would be a far more prosaic place. A house without music is missing a vital dimension.

LEFT: *The telephone is intrusive, but we can choose the quality of its tone and adjust its volume.* RIGHT: *Music on display — big speakers need not always be disguised.*

RIGHT: *Many factors serve to give a house its distinctive sounds, from the people and pets who inhabit it, to the materials of which it is constructed. Here, a dog snores gently as familiar footsteps modulate from soft wooden boards to hard stone flags.*

FAR RIGHT: *Every wooden staircase has its own unique signature tune of tiny echoes, creaks and groans, just as every person has a characteristic foot-fall as they climb it.*

Cookery creates a small orchestra of sound effects, from the alien ping of a microwave to the timeless beat of whisking, pounding and grinding that takes us back to childhood kitchens. Quality of sound depends closely on quality of implement – a metal spoon scraping on a cheap aluminium saucepan can set the teeth on edge just like infamous fingernails on a blackboard.

SIXTH

SENSE

So far in this book we have considered each of the senses that pertain to our physicality – the five channels through which we perceive and enjoy the world surrounding us, the ways in which we recognize our existence. Without our senses, life would lose all meaning, all possibility of interaction. We would be like those disembodied brains of science-fiction, suspended in glass domes, with their artificially simulated voices – a haunting image of a life-form for whom experience could only exist in pure abstraction.

As already discussed in the introduction, a heightened awareness of each of our senses provides a new calculus particularly suited for designing the places in which we live. Once we have accorded importance, not necessarily equal, to our senses of smell, touch, hearing and taste, we are less likely to be subject to the tyranny of the visual and auditory as fed to us through the omnipresent media which rely on it for their impact; television, the printed page, and the computer screen – none of which engage more than two of our senses.

Some might say that the so-called 'sixth sense' is no more than a *sophisticated amalgam* of our other five – with, perhaps, the added ingredients of knowledge and experience. An apparently inexplicable dislike might, for example, be due to a combination of a barely discernible but repugnant smell and a bad association faintly recalled. Whatever its components, we think our sixth sense sufficiently significant to give it a variety of names.

Instinct, gut-feeling, intuition – we are all aware of an extra-sensory dimension, elusive but undeniable. Beyond the rational, it helps us make judgements that don't always conform to rhyme or reason. Falling in love is a function of our sixth sense, whether with a person, a painting or a place to live. When it comes to making those decisions which have a direct bearing on our *emotional well-being*, it is at its most potent, which is why we should attend to it with care when choosing and shaping our territory to make a home.

Home is one of the most emotive words in any language. To be homeless is a tragedy that reaches beyond the simple lack of bed and board. Coming home, leaving home, making yourself at home, feeling home-sick; far more than the simple description of a place, the word evokes *a whole web of emotions* inextricably linked with nationality, tribal belonging, family, loved ones. This is not just any place, but the place where the heart is. Home is also a retreat, a castle, a defence, a symbol and centre of security. Tragedies like incest and abuse are the more terrible because they defile these sacred rules of home.

Home is territory, a private arena, a mini society where you can be prime-minister, monarch and referee. Within the boundaries of your own property, whether rented, owned or borrowed, you are in control. According to zoologist and anthropologist Desmond Morris, 'it is highly likely that private family living-units were present from a very early stage of our human evolution.' In a naturally hierarchical social group, territory provides its owner with a 'spatially limited form of dominance', as Dr Morris puts it, and thereby reduces aggression within the group. Conversely, crimes against territory, whether personal or national, are the most powerful and frequent incitement to violence and war. A burglary is traumatic, not only due to the loss of possessions, which may be irreplaceable, but because it constitutes a violation of territory. On a lesser scale, the door-to-door salesman who thrusts his foot over the threshold is an impostor who risks repulsion.

To have *one's own territory* is an essential ingredient of self-respect for most people. So ingrained is our territorial instinct that we carry it with us even outside the home. In an open-plan office, the desk is taken as territory, marked out with pot-plants or strategically placed waste-paper baskets. Invasions – coming back from holiday to find that someone has been using your space, moving your files and rearranging your things – can cause resentment of primal ferocity.

An important part of consolidating any personal territory is to find ways of marking it as your own. In a car, it may be a personalized number plate; at the office, a photograph or a paperweight. Even temporary territory gets the treatment – the scent on the hotel shelf, the coat over the chair, the bag on the train seat. These are all signals that say 'this is my patch, keep off until you are invited in'.

In the spaces in which we live, we are at optimal liberty to make our own marks, marks that serve the dual purpose of name-tag and display. The image of where we live, like the image of the car we drive and the clothes we wear, is a sign language that is hard to ignore. The very area we choose to inhabit – *urban, suburban or rural* – and the style of building, the precise locus of our territory, already expresses something about ourselves, our status, aspirations and values, even before anyone steps through the door.

Unlike cars and clothes, which we cannot avoid displaying in front of strangers, the interiors of our houses are a more private code, reserved for the eyes of a privileged few. Not content with the purely functional aspects of territory as personal space, we find the need to use it to say something about ourselves with the taste and arrangement of its finer details. These are messages it is impossible not to send; even a refusal to decorate or embellish is personal information. Le Corbusier doggedly resisted the personal in the design of his interiors, preferring to style his furnishings as 'equipment', but his choice of lab jars as vases is just as revealing as the most fanciful Meissen. The 'conspicuous austerity' of minimalism is as powerful a statement about self as is a home crammed with knick-knacks.

Interior decoration is an opportunity for *self-expression in three dimensions*, an art form available to all and practised by everyone. But like all arts, it must strike a balance between striving for a particular effect on a particular audience and the provision of a more personal, even selfish, gratification. An interior designed purely for show, to impress the right people with the right messages, is rarely a comfortable place to live.

Although we may sometimes ignore our own intuition for fear of revealing ignorance or bad taste in the decoration of our homes, we are generally better at using it when making the larger decision of selecting the space we want to inhabit (assuming we have the luxury of any choice in the matter). There are inevitably many practical exigencies dictating where we decide to live – proximity to work and school, economics – but within those limitations there is usually a choice to be made.

Some houses instantly feel like potential homes. You may hate the current decor, bemoan the lack of a fourth bedroom, sigh at the size of the garden, but there is something about the atmosphere of the house, some *intangible essence*, that makes you feel welcome. Despite its disadvantages, this is a house in which you sense you can be comfortable. The converse is equally true. A bad atmosphere in a house can be a powerful and puzzling experience – perhaps it is too dark, has an alien smell or a cold echo; or perhaps it is something more impalpable – the aura of past tragedies. It may not be possible either to explain or articulate the problem, but the feeling of wrongness persists. Old houses often have particularly strong atmospheres, good and bad, as if the walls and floorboards have literally soaked up some of the breath of the past lives they have been witness to.

In a more superstitious age, many precautions were habitually taken to foster *a favourable atmosphere* in the home. Tokens of good fortune were built into the fabric of a house (shoes, for example, ancient symbols of luck, are sometimes found bricked into old chimney breasts), or charms and talismans used to ward off witches and evil spirits. Horseshoes were nailed to front doors, the two ends uppermost so that the good luck wouldn't 'run out' of them; garlic was thought efficacious against witches.

The impulse to invoke greater powers to ensure that a home is a happy and fortunate place is found in every culture. The Romans took great care to pay appropriate honour to their household gods, the Lares and Penates who presided over their dwellings and domestic concerns. Hindu homes incorporate a shrine to a god specially chosen to be their particular guardian, and Buddhists likewise reserve a place for an image of the Buddha and the burning of incense.

The most extensive and codified system of spiritual household insurance must be the ancient Chinese art of feng shui, a complex philosophy that covers every aspect of interior design and promises to maximize good fortune by the auspicious arrangement of furnishings. According to this system, bad feng shui can be caused by a number of physical properties often associated with shapes in the material world. Corners and angles, for example, may emit *shar chi* (translated as 'killing breath') and must be shrouded with plants or palliated with wind chimes. A spiral staircase may also be dangerous, symbolizing a cork-screw boring through a building. Carpet it in red and you are exacerbating its negative power with a symbolic flow of blood.

Although some of the tenets of feng shui may seem fanciful, even simplistic, the aim of living in harmony with the environment by utilizing the earth's energy lines in order to ensure balance between the forces of nature, is a profound and serious one. And while Westerners may feel out of tune with the cultural symbolism that informs its precepts, its attempts to counter bad feelings by using the positive influences of *good proportions*, control of natural light, and landscaping are all ideas we can learn from. Feng shui goes much deeper than aesthetics in its attention to invisible energies. Listening to our own sixth sense makes the same priority.

Listening to our sixth sense and reacting to the atmosphere of a place is important. To keep listening to it as we choose paint colours and curtains seems to come less naturally. Partly, as has already been said, we are endlessly bombarded with other peoples' ideas, presented to us as if ideals. Partly, we may be persuaded to adopt too high a standard of finish, producing an over-decorated, brittle effect. To utilize our sixth sense most effectively we need to side-step the more trivial influences of fashion and marketing in order more clearly to 'feel' what we like.

In truth, only hermits can escape peer group pressure. We are all aspirational and, however eccentric and individual we imagine our tastes to be, we are all under the irresistible influence of a zeitgeist. As historian Peter Thornton points out in his scholarly survey of interior decoration from 1620 to 1920, there is a 'period eye' which informs the arrangement of domestic spaces such that it is possible for the tutored closely to date a room from its appearance alone. In terms of interior decoration, the 'period eye' can, he says, be characterized by the 'density of pattern and arrangements' it finds most pleasing.

At the time Peter Thornton was writing, in 1983, the 'period eye' was tuned to appreciate far more 'density' than it is as we reach the end of the millennium. The country house style was all the rage with its layered accumulations, its salad of chintzes, stripes and toiles. Today, the fashionable interior is pared down; space is again appreciated for its own sake. We are directed towards certain materials – concrete, glass, hardwood, steel, plastic – as if they were a mantra of the modern.

Having *confidence in our own tastes* (and they are usually plural) is not necessarily easy. When free from the persuasions of advertising and class-mates, children generally have fairly certain ideas about what they do and do not like. Show them a Klee or an Auerbach and, unaware of any intellectual or cultural status these artists may hold, they will either *smile in appreciation* or turn up their noses. Although we cannot hope perfectly to recapture such childlike ingenuity, awareness of 'why' we are attracted to certain effects in interior design can help ward against the kind of trendiness that may go against our own grain. The mini may well be 'in' again but if you don't have the legs for it, it's best ignored.

An interior is like an outer skin, a shell, the beauty and originality of which is a direct reflection of the personality of its inhabitant. Like clothing, it is a wordless language. But while we can change our clothes three times a day if we wish, and the colour of our hair once a week, experimenting, dressing up and down to suit our mood, to change the decor of a room is a more labour-intensive and expensive exercise. We can, and do, move things around. We can change curtains and add rugs, *introduce new colours* with flowers and cushions. We can do a lot of fiddling and fine tuning, but refitting a bathroom or a kitchen, or even deciding our bed or sofa is neither attractive nor comfortable, entails major expense. It is important when planning an interior that the bare bones, the shapes and materials, the flooring and finishes are

choices that give us the kind of personal pleasure that goes beyond the desire to make an effect and impress our friends.

In some ways, this has never been more difficult. We are obsessed by surface appearance, in awe of style. Designers are media gods – their clothes, gardens and homes the subject of endless scrutiny, held up as examples of all that is *desirable and good.* We have become a nation of plagiarists, seeking to imitate the powerful cues we see on the television in advertisements and life-style programmes and poring over other peoples' bathrooms in expensive magazines.

Style and fashion is heady stuff – we all fall victim to its charms – we all make mistakes and find ourselves in boxes where we can't be ourselves. But, as proposed in the introduction to this book, there is another way to plan our homes, referring to and relying on our senses. By considering all of them, including our sixth sense or instinct, we immediately vitiate the tendency to the derivative to which the various media make us so vulnerable.

Pictures and moving images are inspiring, good visual design is important, but in order to enjoy our homes in all their dimensions – as the place where we can be closest to the people we love, as a retreat from work and the outside world, as territory where we can be fully sensually expressed – we must start to live in a way that accords as much respect to our other senses as to our eyes.

This is something we can all do – and can only do for ourselves; no outside professional, no interior designer, however intimately acquainted with our personal tastes, can stand in for the information of our own bodies. We may require help and advice, we may need others to put our own ideas into practice, but *if we respond to our senses* and take their preferences fully into account, we need no other guide than ourselves.

All the interiors that have been photographed for this book have the good looks that translate well onto a page. But, if you could walk into the pictures, *lay your head against the cushions,* feel the wooden decking beneath your bare feet, hold your hands up to the reassuring warmth of the fire, lie back in the deepest of baths, simply experience living in any one of these rooms, you would enjoy the sense of sharing and participating in another person's interpretation of *sensual living.* Some elements would afford you as much pleasure as they do its owner, others might not appeal. The challenge is to create your own palace of the senses – a home that is a refuge full of comfort, the kinds of comfort that you personally most enjoy.

RIGHT: *A rosy light filters through diaphanous curtains in a room composed of complementary pastels and gentle textures. Garden flowers, loosely arranged, add a flourish of vibrant red. The effect is both peaceful and harmonious. Eyes are drawn towards the trio of colours in this corner, which also beckons the body with its softly upholstered chair.*

Seen in its entirety, this London living-room, with high windows at front and back, makes a passage for sunlight. White-painted floor and ceiling maximize the sense of brightness and space, sandwiching the sorbet-sweet hues of gauzy curtains, walls and upholstery. Glass bottles, like giant boiled sweets, line up on the mantelpiece; a downy blanket lies across a white linen covered arm; flowers bring their own sweetness; a crystal chandelier adds a note of glorious decadence. Here is a feminine concoction that avoids the saccharine through the simple use of space and the strong, unadorned lines of its furniture.

LEFT: *We are likely to spend more waking time naked in a bathroom than in any other room, making the choice of surfaces particularly pertinent. Here, the glassy-cool tiles and shiny steel fittings, which give this room its air of clean efficiency, are lifted from the clinical to the luxury by the ample folds of snowy towels, the padded bench, also wrapped in towelling, and the rubber flip-flops which await clean feet. A louvred wooden shutter provides privacy and controls the flow of sunlight.*

RIGHT: *Even a toothbrush can be beautiful, pleasing to eye and hand as well as teeth. Details like the raffia trim on a cotton towel can alert the senses to transform everyday routines into habitual indulgences.*

PREVIOUS PAGE: *In an all-white bedroom, texture and form take precedence, and the dark curves of a metal bed-frame stand out like ink on a creamy page. Piled high with cool cotton sheets, feather pillows, and pale, woollen blankets, the bed offers contrasts for the skin as well as warmth and support for the body. An antique mirror propped next to the curtainless window brings the smooth sparkle of glass and the added brightness of reflected light, while its carved decoration, thrown into relief by the bare white walls which frame it, makes a pattern of shadows.*

A satin shoe, a silk jumper, a limestone floor; more than a beautiful image, these are materials

of seductive allure, providing sensations of softness and smoothness, hardness and coldness, warmth

and comfort. They are tactile pleasures, anticipated visually, enjoyed by the skin. As babies and young

children, free from the constrictions of modesty, we revel in nakedness and the brush of different

textures against bare body. As adults, we can choose the fabrics that clothe us to experience those

same pleasures, whether the skim of slippery silk or the hot hug of knitted wool.

LEFT: *Shades of pale in a little girl's bedroom, sunny and feminine. The swirling curlicues of the antique iron cot have been padded at both ends to make a soft lining against the hard metal, like the moss and feathers that insulate a twiggy nest. Children love to feel well-wrapped and enclosed in their beds, burrowing under quilts and duvets, seeking security as well as warmth.*

ABOVE: *During the day – the same little girl makes a sunny verandah her playroom.*

High-maintenance, unforgiving, light-reflecting, white is the colour of cleanliness and purity. The discipline of white informs everything in this pristine kitchen from walls, to work-surfaces to crockery. Satin-brushed steel in strips along the cupboard doors and panels behind the cooker provides a contrast of colour and texture and also contributes to the air of efficiency and hygiene. Sterility is avoided by the beauty of form in the chaste, functional shapes that line the shelves. Far from clinical, the room feels calm, a quiet arena waiting to play host to the colours and clatter of cookery.

A private indoor swimming pool – the ultimate aqueous luxury in any cold climate. Built in the basement of a large house, the design is utterly simple with plain, white walls and pale stone flooring – a huge, heated towel rail the only furnishing. Against this neutral background, the colour of the water is accentuated and heightened by the bright cobalt of the mosaic tiling, beckoning bare feet slowly to descend those underwater steps or to dive straight in. Lack of added colour and ornament again serve to concentrate both mind and body on the sensuous experience of the water itself.

LEFT: *A comfortable family sitting room uses shape and colour to establish a gentle geometry. Chairs and sofa combine strong forms without sacrificing comfort and support; their arrangement on an island of thick carpet is both attractive and sociable, inviting conversation and contact – a place to relax and interact. The unusual planes and angles of the architecture are drawn into the patchwork of shapes with shades of the same blues and greens that link furniture and flooring. The virtues of asymmetry are emphasized by the off-centre arrangement of three simple black and white prints.*

ABOVE: *An etiolated green glass bottle framed by an unusually-shaped aperture makes a cubist still-life that appears to defy perspective. The organic curves of the glass are a striking visual foil to the straight lines and sharp corners around it.*

Light pours into a kitchen where polished marble provides smooth, heat-resistant practicality and the monochrome beauty of its random grain. The contrast between the mineral –

polished rock and shiny metal – and the organic, makes a visual feast.

The texture and brightness of simple, fresh foods appear all the more vibrant for the bleached sheen of their surroundings – the fragile crunch of fresh, vibrantly green chicory seems extra tender when cupped by the hard and glossy steel of its container.

The mosquito net is a happy combination of the practical and pretty. Such is its appeal, both aesthetic and evocative, that it has been adopted as a purely decorative effect in cold

climates where a mosquito bite is about as likely as a hot-water bottle is necessary. In this château in France it serves both purposes in a bedroom that is feminine without the frills.

A corridor in the same château is lit by sunlight sieved through fine yellow gingham, a warm hue picked up in the gentle paint colours of corn, and complemented by a soft sky blue.

Pattern and shape are already provided by the architecture of domed ceiling and curving door panelling.

As soon as daylight dwindles, we need to make our own light, and its quality and intensity will become the single most potent decorative effect in any room. Fluorescent strips or harsh overhead lighting are as unflattering to spaces as to faces; side lights, low lights and candle light are infinitely kinder. At night, lighting is ambience; to play with its effects is to experiment with atmosphere. These simple lanterns not only provide the warm glow of a flame, they make a moving light-show, casting soft-edged shadows and patterns that modulate with the slightest breeze, or float across walls as they sway suspended from their wire hooks.

Every room needs a focus: in a bedroom, the bed; in a bathroom, the bath; in

a kitchen, the cooker. In this living room, the focus, at least in winter, is not that electric

substitute, the television, but the ancient and eternally fascinating element, fire.

Eyes are magnetized by its light and movement, bodies are drawn towards its warmth

and, in case anyone should doubt its status in the room, its mantelpiece is the platform

for three striking objects, a bold triumvirate of dark shapes. Without sacrificing an iota

of visual impact, everything in this room of earthy colours and soft textures is arranged

for physical comfort. Lights by chair and sofa are an invitation to sit with a book,

a suede shawl smells as good as it feels.

PREVIOUS PAGE:

*Dramatic decorative
effects can be achieved
with minimal
ingredients. Four basic
elements comprise the
impact of this space –
a painting, a lamp-
shade, a vase of flowers
and a table and chairs.
The success of their
grouping relies on both
homogeneity and
antithesis. Harmony
between these different
pieces results from their
closeness in colour –
a palette of browns,
yellows and ochres
that are more
complementary than
contrasting. Visual
disturbance and
excitement come from
the differences in form.*

FAR LEFT: *Here is a place where every one of our senses could find itself engaged. Coloured glass pierces a pretty picture in a blank wall, mediating the light that falls through it. The same green glass takes different forms on the table. The forest browns of polished furniture and floorboards are echoed in the low-hanging shade. There is a sharp, clean scent of lemons, like a foretaste of their sourness, and a warmer, softer smell of wax polish.*

LEFT: *The mathematical precision of a chair back finds a match in the harlequin fabric covering a cushion.*

A room in an old French château transformed by colour, pattern and light. Stone walls and floor and the low-vaulted ceiling have a potentially cold, monastic feel which has been converted from the chill to the welcome with a wash of sunny paint, antique furniture of comfortable solidity and bold design, and the gentle brightness of a dozen candles.

Just as the chill has been banished by the warmth of colour, so any sense of claustrophobia one might feel cocooned by these thick stone walls has been converted into cosy charm.

Rustic earthenware is in keeping with a style that has a slightly rough-hewn plainness, both medieval and modern.

LEFT: *Wood, metal, marble, stone, ceramic, glass – this is a kitchen that looks as though it means business, where design would appear to have taken a step back in favour of efficiency – with its double sinks and double taps, its huge glass-fronted fridge and expanse of work surface. But this is also a room that you can enjoy being in; there is space, there is light, and there is the pleasure of stone underfoot, the cool of marble surfaces, and the oily slide of a perfectly fitting wooden drawer. The perceived strength of materials also brings its own beauty – a blending of natural monotones against which the colour of fresh basil gains extra radiance. This is a kitchen where you can cater for fifty, bringing its stern, no-nonsense furnishings alive with the smells, the sounds and the colours for which it is the ideal stage.*

OVERLEAF: *Eating or drinking in the bath is a strangely sybaritic experience which seems to add up to more than the sum of two everyday physical pleasures. The design of this flat in Rome positively encourages such hedonism; its deep bath, which appears bottomless owing to its lining of black mosaic tiles, is an extension of the kitchen, with a wooden table that slides up and down its length to maximize work surface and facilitate watery feasting. The temptation to lie back with a cappuccino and croissant every morning must be irresistible – and no need to sweep up the crumbs afterwards (although sushi might be more in tune with the pared down styling). Floating candles add fuel to the aura of Oriental mystery. Privacy is afforded by thin, white blinds, like Japanese paper screens.*

Good design is not necessarily timeless – this undulating sofa is obviously Regency and very much of its time, but the visual pleasure it affords goes far beyond its associations of elegance, or its status as antique. Silhouetted against the light from a high window, it has the presence of a piece of sculpture. On either side, the pair of vases allow light through, as do the translucent petals of the lilies. The curves of the glass and flowers pick up those of the sofa and contrast with the angularity of their architectural back-drop. Comfort and comeliness sit side by side.

LEFT: *In a modern Los Angeles house, the flow of open-plan space can be subtly interrupted by these sliding doors. Dividing the kitchen from the rest of the living area, like the screens in traditional Japanese homes, the doors allow one to cut off sound and sight but let the light continue its journey through the house via a series of square windows glazed with frosted glass. By adjusting the width of space between doors from a wide aperture to a narrow slot, the character of the vista between rooms can be changed dramatically.*

RIGHT: *White tulips have a translucence and simplicity of form, which combine with the strong bend of their stems and spike of their leaves to make living designs in a vase.*

RIGHT: *Another*
Los Angeles house in
a completely different
mood. The wooden
structure with its
primitive planking and
beams has been unified
with white paint –
a bleaching out of
colour that has spread
over the furniture,
ornaments and even
book covers. White also
works to tone down
the fanciful curlicues
of cupboard and table,
leaving them lacy and
light instead of
overbearing. The effect
is fresh and informal
but not unsophisticated.

The chandelier with its
twisted wires and
tarnished metal flowers,
like a charming relic
from an ancient
wedding, makes a leafy
pattern against its pale
background.

This beach house on the island of St Barts in the Caribbean makes the best of its setting by minimizing the distinction between outdoors and indoors; white-painted floorboards spread through rooms out onto verandas. Windows become doors, open to draw in the breeze and its papery rustle as it shakes the palm leaves. The low swish of waves breaking on fine, level sand, is a constant background – the bass notes which sound their endless rhythm beneath the tunes of wind, sea-birds and bare feet on floorboards. Wooden furniture makes shapes of dramatic darkness against the light; colour is in the ever-changing azure sea and sky.

RIGHT: *A huge bathroom where scale and space equal luxury. Extended in the middle of its cool, white simplicity, is an ample bath, floating like a boat or a cradle, inviting you to sink into its warmth.*

OVERLEAF: *This white wooden house sits in the middle of the garden and has the charm of an elegant garden shed or grown-up Wendy house. The discipline of whiteness gives anything that breaks the rule extra prominence; pale stripes of upholstery running counter to the stripes of the chair backs, and the dark line that circles the moon of the table, stand out like cracks in snow.*

A panel of tongue and groove planking lines one wall of this kitchen. Unlike stone, brick or plaster, wood is one of the natural materials we think of as 'warm' and 'soft', and, in comparison with other building materials, it is. Using it to line a room promotes a sense of cosiness and insulation. Here, instead of the mouldings or panels that characterize antique room panelling, there is the restrained stripe of match-boarding providing pattern and texture. The mauve flowers and lemony-green paintwork are near complementary colours — violet and yellow are on opposite sides of the colour wheel — and work particularly well together. The draped chair and the thick mohair blanket with its broad satin trim, explore the same colour in different textures.

*This large bed sits in
the middle of a modest
bedroom, filling the
space with its
comfortable bulk and
facing windows which
open straight onto the
sea. Like the bath
shown in a previous
picture (see page 145),
its position in the room
is not anchored to any
of the walls. This gives
it both status as the
room's central piece and
lets it float, more ship
than boat, its dark,
theatrical shape
surrounded by seamless
white. The tall mirror
on one wall makes
another window onto
a twin space.*

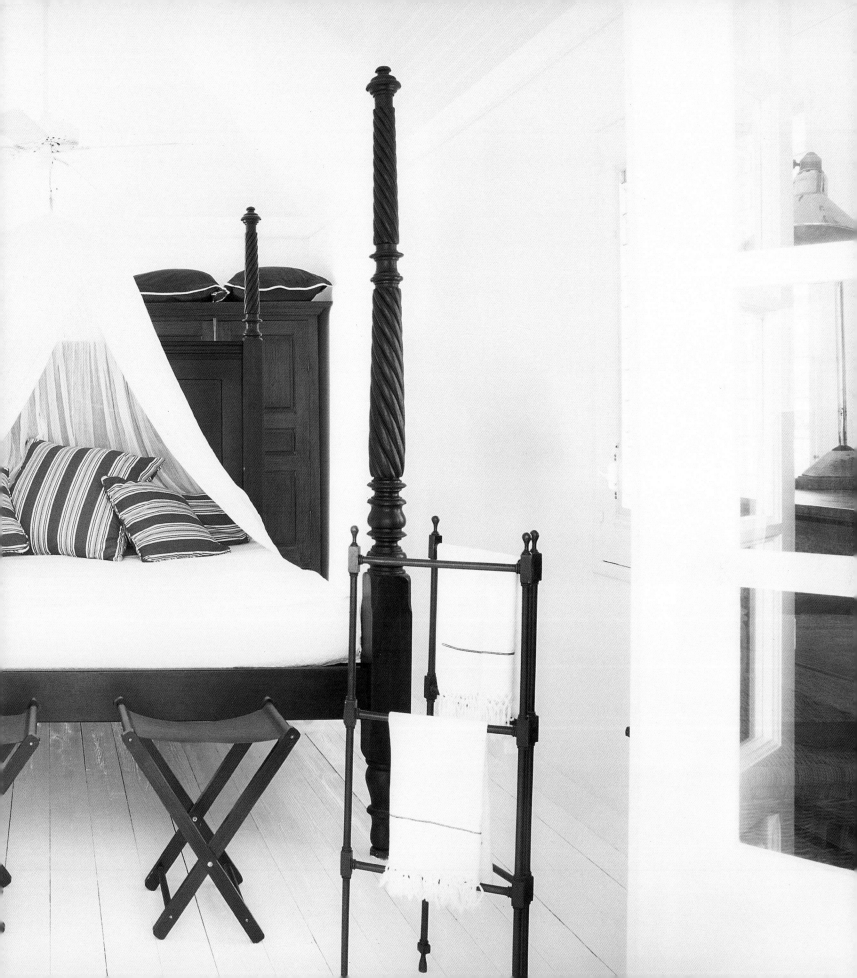

White and pale green give this house its clean atmosphere. In the bedroom, white predominates on all surfaces but one, on the sheets, upholstery, and on the muslin curtains. A glance inside the owner's wardrobe reveals more green and white, like the shoes and jumper over the chair. Favourite colours seem to come from nowhere but our preferences for them persist in our choice of clothes, remaining independent of fashion. These favourites are colours we like to live with but are not always brave enough to paint on our walls.

RIGHT: *A plant is a living sculpture, growing, flowering, forming seed heads, never precisely the same from day to day. A scented plant adds another dimension to the visual pleasure.*

FAR RIGHT: *In a room blessed with good proportions and architectural interest, the lack of clutter is calming rather than bland. Maximum contrast is provided by the shiny black of the floor crisply joining walls. The daybed, with its silky blanket, looks like the perfect place to meditate; an empty space in which to empty the mind.*

This Sydney apartment mixes an eclectic collection of furniture which unreservedly mixes the antique with the modern. Unified by the monochrome colour scheme, wittily picked up in chessboard cushions, the visual comparison between the eighteenth-century French armchair with its gilding and carving, and the pop-art, amoebic curves of the black swivel chair, are at once stark in terms of sensibility and materials, and subtle in terms of form and function; both chairs share the aim of giving comfort and support, both use protuberant curves to provide it. The mix of furnishings challenges the eye; the restrained palette of black, white and cream, and the gently filtered light, soothe it.

Page references in italics refer to photographs

A
acoustics, good/bad 86
air quality 30
air-conditioning 30
animals: noises 85
    skin 30, 46
aromatherapy 21
Art Deco 74
asymmetry 77, 116–17
B
babies: and water 35
    crying 85
    exploring touch 30, 109
    feeding 53
    smell of 16
background noise 84, 85, 143
bad smells, masking 25
bathing 36
    by candlelight 72
    sound of 85
bathrooms 106–7, 134–5, 144–5
    heating 46
    planning 100
    smells in 17
    texture in 37
beach house 142–3
beaches 35, 37
    picnics on 58
    shade on 65
beauty 80
    human need for 65
    'serpentine line of' 77
beauty treatments 30
bedding/blankets 37, 42–3, 102–3, 104–5, 152–3, 155
    tactility 30, 33, 37
bedrooms 104–5, 110, 120–1, 150–1
    smells in 25
    textures 30
bells 85
black 73, 81
Blind Girl, The (Millais) 65
body scents 16, 25
body-wraps 30
breast milk 51–3
C
candles 72, 130–1, 134–5, 141
    scented 17, 25
carpets 46, 116–17
    effect on noise 86

ceilings: scale and 74–7, 102–3, 130–1
    sound systems in 88–9
    sound-proofing 86
central heating 30
chairs 14, 37, 43–6, 65, 101, 116–17, 128–9
    as retreat 77
chandeliers 72, 141
cheese 51, 56–7
children: exploring touch 30, 44, 109, 110
    flooring for 46
chocolate 23, 52, 58
clothing: home as 80
    tactility 31, 32, 40, 46, 108–9
    white/black 74
coffee 23, 52, 54–5
cologne, old-fashioned 23
colour 65, 72–3, 121
    as visual focus 66–7, 76, 77
    complementary 73, 126–7, 148–9
    contemporary 100, 101
    contrasting 77–80, 112–13
    cosiness and 74–7
    iridescent 72–3
    monochrome 68, 132–3, 156–7
    see also black; white
    personal choice 73, 99, 100, 152–3
    'saturation'/'lightness' 73
    secondary 73
    symbolism of 73
colour wheel 73
conservatories 72
Constable, on beauty 80
continental breakfast 54–5
contrasts: textural 46, 47
    visual 77–80, 112–13
cookery 51, 58
    sound of 85, 94–5
cotton 31, 37, 43, 65
country house style 100
country noises 86
curlicues, rococo 77
curtains 37, 99, 100, 101
    as sound-proofing 86
cushions 34, 35, 37–43, 42–3, 75, 77, 100
D
damask 37
dance and rhythm 86, 91
dislikes, reasons for 98

distemper 74
drinks: smell of 23, 54–5
    taste of 50, 52
E
eating: disorders 58
    habits 51–3
    out/outdoors 58
emotion: about home 98
    colour and 73
    music and 91
    smell and 21–3
eyes, sensitivity of 65
F
fabrics 37, 129, 146–7
    chintz 80
    choosing 37
    fake fur 34
    light and 65
    natural 37, 42–3
    satin 36–7
    scent/medication-infused 37
    seasonal changes 37–43
    synthetics 37
    tactility 37, 40
feng shui 99
fire 25, 78
flagstones 25, 46
floor coverings: effect on scale 74
    effect on sound 86, 92
    natural fibres 46
    see also specific types
floors 25, 128
    tactility 46
    white 74, 140, 142–3
flowers 16, 17, 21, 62–3, 65, 101, 102–3, 126–7, 154
    colour 73, 76, 100, 139, 148–9
    smell of 16–21, 17, 20, 154
    tactility 31
focal points 66–7, 76, 77, 117, 124–5
food 14, 27, 51
    comfort food 53
    fads 58
    identifying flavours 51, 52
    texture of 38–9, 119
    see also cookery; drinks
fountains/pools/waterfalls 35, 85
Fowler, John 74
fresh air 25, 30
fruit 19, 21, 24, 57
    preference for 51
    smell of 21, 24
full-spectrum light 72

fur: coats 30, 34
    fake 30, 35
    see also pets
furniture/furnishings 58, 126–7, 130–1
    as 'equipment' 74, 99
    effect on scale 74–7
    painted 140, 146–7
    selecting and placing 77–80, 98–9, 156–7
    tactility 30, 37, 42–3, 46
G
'glance curve' 77
glass 34, 72, 102–3, 117, 128
    frosted 65
    see also mirrors; windows
good fortune tokens 99
good/bad atmosphere 99
'green rooms' 73
grooming, social 30
'grooming talk' 30
H
Hagia Sophia, Istanbul 74
hairdressing 30
Hampton Court: carvings 65
    sound-proofing 86
hand shaking 30
heaven, definitions of 51
Heaven Room, Burghley 65
herbs 21, 25, 51
    smell of 21, 25
    strewn 25
Hogarth, on line 77
home, what it is 98
household gods 99
household noise 85–6
houses: choosing 98–9
    effect of scale 74
    made of glass 72
    smell of 25
    water features 35
I
ice cream 51, 59
incense 21, 25
interior decorators/decoration 80
    self-expression through 98–100
    sixth sense and 99–100
K
Kandinsky, on colour 73
Kings College Chapel, Cambridge 74
kissing, social 30
kitchens 58, 134–5
    planning 100

smell of 25, 26
textural contrasts *47, 112–13, 118, 132–3*
utensils/equipment *43*, 46, 87, 94–5
Kiwant Ti 21

L
laundry, smell of fresh *17, 22*
lead paint 74
leather *14, 18*, 37
upholstery *32, 34*, 37
light, artificial 72, *122–3, 124–5, 126–7, 130–1*
effect of wrong type 72
fluorescent 72, *123*
light, natural: architectural use 65, *118, 136–7*
controlling *64*, 65, 99, 101, 121
effect of lack of 65, 72
see also sunlight
white and 74
lighting designers 72
limewash 74
linen *22, 35*, 37, 43, 58, 74, *102–3*
log fires 25
Louis XV, King 21
love: acts of 53–8
falling in 98
look of 65

M
'machine for living' (Le Corbusier) 74, 99
manicures 30
marble 46, *118*
massage 30, 36
Matisse, on colour 73
Maugham, Syrie 74
memory, smell and 21–3
meringue 25, 51
metal 36, *43*
miasmas 16
Middle Ages: floor covering 46
food fashions 51
window coverings 65
mirrors *70*, 74, *150–1*
Modernist architecture 35–6, 74
Morris, Desmond 30, 98
Morris, William 80
mosquito netting *120–1*
Munch, on colour 73
music 85, 86–91, *88–9, 91*
as mood control 91
behaviour/attitudes and 91
muslin 65, *120–1, 152–3*

N
Nero, Emperor 21
Newton, light studies 72–3
noise: of life 85
unexpected 85
'novelty cuisine' 51

O
offering 53–8
'office sickness' 72
oils: aromatic 21
colour film 72–3
open-plan living 74, *138*
offices 98
ornaments/objects 79, *102–3*
choosing and placing 77–80, 80, 98–9, *136–7*
tactility 41, 46
visual impact *66–7, 117, 124–5*

P
paintings/drawings 65, 73, 100
looking at 77
Pascal, on symmetry 77
pastry baking *54–5*
pearls 46
perception: colour 65, 73
smell and 21–3
sound 85
Perfume (Suskind) 16
perfumes/scents 16, 21, 25, 37
'period eye' 100
pets, stroking 30, *34*
picnics 58
plants, scented 21
see also flowers; fruits; herbs
pomanders 25
porcelain 46, *47*
Proust 21, 23, 65

R
rainbow 65, 73
reflections 65, *70*
sound 86
restaurants and cafés 58
music in 91
retreat, personal 77
rose-water 21
rugs and matting 25, 30, *34*, 37, 46, 74, 100
bathrooms 37
over floorboards 46
rush light 72

S
sand 30, *37*
Scream, The (Munch) 73
self-expression 98–9

showers, cold 36, *36*
shutters/screens *64*, 65, 74, *138*
as soundproofing 86
silk 37
sitting room *116–17*
'sixth sense', what it is 98
skin 30
effect of candlelight 72
maintenance of 30
smell of 16
texture and 37, 46
sky-lights 72
smell of 16, *19*, 23, 25
soap bubbles 72
sofas *32, 42–3, 68–9*, 74, 100, *116–17, 136–7*
'solar' 65
sound: listing favourite 85
natural 85
selective hearing 85
what it is 85
space: empty *155*
illusion of 74, *102–3, 130–1*
spices 58
spoken word 85, 86
staircases *93*
stale smells 25
stone 25, *43*, 46, *92, 130–1*
straight lines 77
suede *22–3*, 37, *124–5*
sunlight 65, *68–9, 102–3*, 121
sweet tooth 51–3
swimming, naked 35
swimming pools 35, *114–15*
symmetry 77

T
taste of 51, *51*
taste/tastes: complementing texture *56–7*
confidence in personal 100
identifying 51, *52*
sense of smell and 52
taste buds 51
telephones 85, *90*
temperature: colour 73
touch and 46
territorial instinct 98
texture *32–3*, 46, *47, 101*
architectural uses 36
complementing taste *56–7*
effect on colours and light *71, 75, 81*
see also clothing; upholstery
Thornton, Peter 100

tobacco smoke 25
touching, avoidance of 30
towels *17*, 30, 37, 43, 44–5, 74, *106, 107*
traffic noise 85
trompe l'oeil, Port Lympne 65

U
underfloor heating 46
upholstery *14*, 25, *32, 34*, 36–7, 74, 100
importance of texture 37
reflecting colours *75*
smell of *14*
see also chairs; fabrics; sofas

V
vegetables *26, 36, 38–9*
velvet 37, 43
Venetian blinds 65
Versailles 65
perfume rules 21

W
waiting rooms 65
walking barefoot *37*, 46
walls: fabric-covered 86
white 65, 74
water 35–6, *36, 59, 114–15*
sound of 85, *143*
white 65, *70, 71*, 73–4, *102–3, 112–13, 114–15, 139, 140, 142–3, 144–5, 146–7, 152–3*
drawing room 74
'magnolia' 73
symbolism of 73
whitewash 74
windows 65, 72
coverings *64*, 65, 72
view through 72
wood
bare and polished 25, 36, *128*
carvings 65
effect of light 65
effect on sound *92, 93*
painted *140, 146–7, 148–9*
wool 37, *42–3*
floor coverings 37, 46
smell of 25
tactility *33, 35*
Woolf, Elsie de 74
work surfaces 46, *112–13, 118, 132–3, 134–5*
Wright, Frank Lloyd
Falling Water 35
use of texture 36
wrist watches 85, *86*

First published in 1998 by
Conran Octopus Limited
37 Shelton Street
London WC2H 9HN

ISBN 1 85029 934 X

Text copyright © Claire Lloyd & Ros Byam Shaw 1998
Photographs copyright © the photographers 1998
Design & layout copyright © Conran Octopus Ltd 1998

COMMISSIONING EDITOR Denny Hemming
SENIOR MANAGING EDITOR Gillian Haslam
ART DIRECTOR Helen Lewis
TYPESETTER Olivia Norton

All rights reserved. No part of this book may be
reproduced, stored in a retrieval system, or transmitted,
in any form or by any means, electronic, electrostatic,
magnetic tape, mechanical, photocopying, recording or
otherwise, without the prior permission in writing of
the publisher.

The right of Claire Lloyd to be identified as Author of
this Work has been asserted by her in accordance with
the Copyright, Designs and Patents Act 1988.

British Library in Cataloguing-in-Publication Data
A catalogue record for this book is available from the
British Library.

Printed in China

Photographic Credits

HANNAH LEWIS: pages 1, 4-5, 14-15, 17 bottom, 18 (shawl and briefcase from Connolly Leather), 19, 20, 21, 22 (selection of old linen from Briony Thomasson), 25, 26, 27, 33, 34-35 (all items from The Stanley Supply Store). 36 bottom, 41, 42 (cushion from The Stanley Supply Store), 43 bottom, 45, 47, 50, 52, 53, 54-55, 56-57, 57, 59 (sunglasses from Connolly Leather), 61, 64, 68, 69, 70, 71, 76, 78, 81, 87, 88-89, 92, 93, 94, 95, 101 (designed by Janie Jackson) , 102-103, 104-105, 108-109, 110, 112 (designed by Annie Stevens), 113, 114, 115, 120, 121, 122-123, 130-131, 132, 133, 134 (architects: Claudio Lazzarini and Carl Pickering), 135, 136-137, 144-145, 148 (designed by Janie Jackson), 149, 152 (designed by Janie Jackson), 153, 154, 155. GEOFF LUNG: pages 6, 13, 17 left, top right and middle right, 24, 29, 32 (architect: Brian Kiernan), 36 top, 37, 40, 43 top and middle, 44, 49, 51, 56, 62-63, 66-67, 75, 77, 79, 84, 86, 90, 91, 106, 107, 111, 116 (architect: Josh Schweitzer), 117, 118 (architect: Iain Halliday), 119, 126-129 (designed by Paul Fortune), 138, 139, 140 (designed by Theadora Van Runkle), 141, 142, 143, 146-147 (designed by Theadora Van Runkle), 150-151, 156-157 (architect: Iain Halliday), 160. ELIZABETH ZESCHIN: pages 2-3, 12, 22-23 middle, 23, 28, 31, 38-39, 48, 60, 82, 83, 96-97, 124, 125.

The extract on page 23 from *In Search of Lost Time: Swann's Way* by Marcel Proust, translated by C K Scott Moncrieff and Terence Kilmartin, is reproduced with kind permission of Chatto & Windus/Vintage.

Author's Acknowledgments

I wish to thank the following people:
Ros Byam Shaw for putting my vision into words; the photographers Hannah Lewis, Geoff Lung and Elizabeth Zeschin; Helen Lewis, Gillian Haslam, Denny Hemming and Leslie Harrington at Conran Octopus for their hard work; my agent, Gillian Young at Lighthouse; my assistants past and present: Kirsty Flanagan, Alison Davies, Sasha Dunn; Domenica More Gordon for her Los Angeles contacts and for being a great friend; Matthew Usmar Lauder for his constant support and unfailing patience.

I am fortunate to have friends with fantastic taste who allowed me into their homes
Isabel and Joseph Ettedgui, Janie Jackson, Stephen and Alisa Marks, Jonathan Reed, Jon and June Summerill, Susan Hipgrave and Edward Waring, Gil Friesen and Louise Barnetson.

Thank you to the following designers and architects:
In Australia Iain Halliday and Brian Kiernan; in Los Angeles Paul Fortune, Josh Schweitzer and Theadora Van Runkle; in Rome Claudio Lazzarini and Carl Pickering; in London Janie Jackson, Jonathan Reed and Annie Stevens.

I would also like to thank the following models:
Tara Owens, Denise Dorrance, Ella Marks, Jack Fletcher and Gigi Ettedgui.